B2

'The Doorstep Baker by Catherine Lloyd-Williams is an inclusive, supportive, encouraging and scrupulously clear recipe book by a Gold award winner of the Free From Food Awards 2023. Motivated to bring her recipes to ordinary people, having gathered many through her career as caterer, baker, and homebaker, she writes with confidence and even includes a section called 'Baking Motivation' for those who may quail before the task! Lloyd-Williams firmly holds the reader's hand through the introductory pages and beyond, leading the apprehensive or sceptical with agility and reassurance to navigate the cliff edge of allergen-aware baking.

She strikes the perfect balance to appeal to novice and established baker, incorporating skilled bread making, free from baking and any non-proficiency in the kitchen: writing how I imagine she would speak, her writing quickly becomes a guide. The fly-leaf quote, about her dad to whom the book is dedicated, sums up the approach of The Doorstep Baker: "It's not about being perfect. It's about enjoying your creations with others."'

Cressida Langlands, CEO, Free From Food Awards, 2024

The Doorstep Baker

You can make all sorts of bread

Catherine Lloyd-Williams

This, my first recipe book, is dedicated to

Dad

*'It's not about being perfect.
It's about enjoying your
creations with others.'*

First Edition 2024 THE DOORSTEP BAKER:
YOU CAN MAKE ALL SORTS OF BREAD
Copyright © Catherine Lloyd-Williams, 2024

Editor: Catherine Lloyd-Williams
Proofreader: Siân Smith
Layout Design: Sami Harrison
Photography: Helen Yandell

A CIP catalogue record for this book is available
from the British Library.

ISBN: 978-1-3999-9232-9

Contents

Introduction   05
    The Sourdough Clean-Up   07
    My Baking Tips   09
    Utensils   13
    Baking Motivation   15

Sourdough Recipes   17
    Sourdough Starter   19
    Classic White Sourdough   23
    '70/30' Wholemeal & White Sourdough   29
    Deep Malthouse Sourdough   31
    Chef's Rye Blend Sourdough   33
    Flavoured Sourdough   35
    See You Later Sourdough   39
    Sourdough Cobs   41
    Sourdough Pizza & Pizza Sauce   45
    Sourdough Focaccia   49
    Herby Sourdough Croutons   52

Dough Recipes   53
    First-Time Focaccia   55
    Inspired Flatbreads   59
    Brioche Burger Buns   63
    One Hundred Per Cent Wholemeal   67
    The Buttie Satisfier – White Tin Loaf   71
    Loaf of Deep Rye   75
    Spelt Bread Rolls   79
    Garlic & Herb Milk Bread Twists   83
    Stuffed Loaf   87
    Maneesh Style Flatbreads   91
    Ciabatta Sticks or Rolls   95
    Sticky Cinnamon Buns   99
    Teacakes for Toasting   103
    Grandma's Leicester Style Fruit Bread   107
    Hot Cross Fruit or Choc Chip Buns   111

Gluten Free   115
    Gluten Free Fluffy Focaccia   117
    Gluten Free Fluffy Loaf   121
    Gluten Free Buckwheat Loaf   125

Index & Acknowledgements   129

Introduction

I adopted the term microbakery for my small homebaking business, The Doorstep Baker. And I like to encourage anyone to be a baker and I believe anyone can bake. I am grateful to have watched and joined in with cooking from scratch alongside my mother from an early age. And I also had a grandmother who trained and worked in catering in the 1930s. I even have her written recipe book, given to me by my dad. So perhaps this foundation helped me to feel confident in baking, even when I wasn't professionally experienced to begin with. And the unsuccessful attempts at baking sourdough and bread happened to me, as I started to learn bread baking.

I have always had a big interest in cookery programmes and books, yet sometimes following a recipe can be open to interpretation. Having made, baked and delivered sourdough, breads, cakes and more for over 4 years, I have gathered experience of how to write recipes for homebakers like me. I have also cooked and baked in professional workplaces, with the simple start point of being a passionate homecook. I want to share the recipes I've developed, to help you in your baking attempts.

This recipe book allows you to get a more direct route to a great result, because I have been through the pitfalls of developing these recipes and made them understandable from a homebaker perspective. I hope you will find joy and calmness in it along the way, as I have. Once you get into the swing of making bread, to your own schedule and demands of life, it will become second nature.

It just takes consistency and a little resilience. Your confidence in baking will grow as your attempts succeed more and more. Please adapt your recipes to your personal taste as you learn them, and don't put unrealistic pressure on yourself to make them perfect. I, like you, am still learning and that means we can make as many mistakes as we like. Just don't let it put you off from trying.

Part of my motivation for running my own microbakery came from wanting to learn about making bread for my family, for my local community and for those with food allergies and intolerances. Before baking for my business and for other businesses, I was a family support worker, and then a project worker for adults with special needs. Previously I had worked in administrative roles and completed a social sciences degree, as a mature student. Having 2 boys at different stages of my life meant I was cooking daily family meals from the age of 21, and before that I enjoyed cooking evening meals for my busy parents and sisters. Whether you cook or bake for yourself or others, with food allergies or not, you will spend a lot of time in the kitchen. I hope you find here some trusty recipes that you can enjoy making and eating together.

I give ingredient alternatives to a recipe, where I have tried and tested it. And where I haven't, I make suggestions. Often these are in relation to plant-based diets and gluten free options. My main focus has been on leaving out peanuts, tree nuts and all of their derivatives. I am a Gold award winner of the 2023 Free From Food Awards, for my classic sourdough loaf, in the nut and peanut free category. I realised an ambition to bring something positive and new to people with tree nut and peanut allergies. But we all have different requirements, so if you are a household who can eat these, add them in where you feel appropriate.

Baking bread has the added advantage of being a mindful action, like painting, exercising or anything that focusses on the action of doing. It brings you to this present moment, where you can just let yourself be absorbed in the creativity of bringing ingredients together. This is a very tactile activity, which can provide valuable moments of solitude and some say it is a spiritual practice. I think my love of the combining, mixing and gloopy nature of it all can be traced back to my life as an under 5. From a very early age I loved to play in the garden with soil and water. When all sisters and my parents were in the house, you could find me outside, crouched over the recessed circles of the drain covers. Puddle-like from the rain. My two simple mixing bowls offering...

Mud pies and mud smiles!
The weight of the world
heavy in the stir,
The stick thick with grainy,
dark promise.
Growing, overflowing, splashing,
and pushing down in the deep.
No what, no but, no why.
Providing peace,
with simple certainty.

I hope you find this feeling in your baking too. Switch off from what is around you and find baking calmness amongst the chaos. And allow yourself to make loads of mess. We are so terrified of mess, but mess-making is part of our primary learning. Learning to bake bread is a gift to yourself for now and a gift to yourself and your loved ones for the future bakes and the meals you will share.

Catherine Lloyd-Williams

The Sourdough Clean-Up

A customer came to see me at a market in Malvern, after buying my sourdough kit and recipe the previous month. It included a pot of The Doorstep Baker rye starter.

His feedback about the recipe was that it was a good recipe to follow and instructed him in all he needed for a first sourdough attempt. He said he'd turned out about 3 decent loaves already. I was very happy to hear the feedback. 'However,' he said, 'it's the sourdough mess afterwards. It doesn't

make me popular in the kitchen at home.' If you've ever made sourdough before, what isn't often mentioned is that the wet mixture of sourdough sticks like a type of glue once dried. It doesn't dissolve easily, so when washing it off hands or utensils it can leave blobs of dough in the sink. But this is something you can worry less about, as I have been learning useful ways to clean up sourdough dough over the years of making it.

The Doorstep Baker

Here are my recommendations for an easier clean-up for you. This equals a happier household, saves time and keeps the plughole and drains clear.

When feeding the starter or making the dough mixture you can use:

- A rubber type spatula to clear down the sides of your starter tub or pot

- A clean eating knife to scrape off the dough from the spatula, back into the starter or dough mix

- A saucer or spoon rest to keep the used utensils in one place and off the worktop for a quicker clean-up

- A plughole cover / protector for any loose dough to be collected and then disposed of into the bin / compost bin

- A silicone dish brush for washing wet dough bowls. This cleans them without clinging on to the dough so much. I found these in large home and craft type stores.

Have an area for used, empty bowls to sit. Scrape off as much wet mixture as you can with a rounded dough scraper.

Then allow them to sit and air dry overnight. You can then use the dough scraper to remove more of the dried on mixture to dispose of or even keep and use as a dehydrated form of starter.

When disposing of the starter, I do not recommend putting it down the plughole.

The options I've used are:

- Use it in a sourdough discard recipe, like the pizza in this book or cookies and brownies

- Give it away – what a great gift for someone to receive!

- Compost it. Place any excess starter in your compost bin and mix it in with leaves and straw. Small amounts at a time would be a good addition to the ecosystem inside there.

- Use biodegradable caddy bags. If you have made way too much and have tried the above options, then place the leftovers in one of these, tie it up and place in general waste. The starter and the bag are both biodegradable.

My Baking Tips

I hope to answer questions here that may come to mind when you're baking any recipe in this book. Writing a recipe book is straightforward at first. But the more I return to writing a recipe, the more questions I anticipate. And it is often the things not said in a recipe that can cause confusion.

Yeast

In this book I use sourdough starter and I use fast action yeast. I use the fast action yeast as it gives you a good rise and is widely available. Other yeasts are available to use. These include dried yeast and fresh yeast. Dried yeasts that are not labelled as fast or instant will need to be activated with warm water or milk to avoid getting clumps of yeast in the dough. You can use the same amount of yeast in the recipe. You may find the dried yeast is slower to rise a dough than the fast yeast. The advantage of dried yeast, compared to fast yeast, is that many contain fewer or no additional additives.

I use gluten free fast action dried yeast in the gluten free recipes. This is available in the 'free from' sections of shops, supermarkets and online. I reluctantly use baking powder in my main gluten free recipes, as I find it helps to avoid the sinking of the baked bread at the end. You can try those recipes without baking powder or with less and see how you get on.

Any opened dried yeast can be stored in an airtight container. Or a sachet can have a bag clip put over the end. Put it in the fridge and keep it for up to 3 months. If you haven't used it in a while and want to test if the yeast is alive, place a little in some tepid water and see if it will froth within a few minutes.

Fresh yeast is also available for use and it is good to crumble this into water, for it to mix evenly into the other ingredients. The amount you would use of fresh yeast needs to be about a third more than the weight of the fast action yeast. Fresh yeast doesn't have the longer shelf life of dried yeasts and will need to be kept in the fridge. It's often available from bakery suppliers online or you may be able to find some local to where you live.

Sticky doughs, kneading styles and proving

Very sticky doughs – use an electric mixer with a dough hook if you have one. It can be done by hand if you don't. The time will just take a little longer. The gluten free recipes are often like cake batter, so an electric hand mixer with beaters is good for these.

Kneading styles – I like to fold the dough over onto the rest of the dough, push with the heel of my hand and lift the dough and slap it near the edge of the worktop. A combination of this is great to get the proteins in the flour going. Basically, what happens is the kneading creates warmth, which activates the proteins in the flour to form gluten strands. This encourages a more elastic dough that grows with good structure in the fermentation stage. You can develop your own way of kneading that encourages the warmth and elasticity.

If you have arthritis or pain, then again use a stand style mixer with a dough hook.

If it's a cold day you can prove your dough in an airing cupboard or somewhere similarly warm. You may even have a proving drawer. Just don't put dough to prove on direct heat, like a radiator or with the oven temperature on. You can use the oven light only though, if your oven has the facility to just turn on the light. The very gentle heat from the bulb is enough, in this enclosed space, to prove your dough that's in its own covered bowl. And remember that on a very hot day your yeasted dough or sourdough will grow a lot faster than usual. This can be a real help to get more recipes made or you may have got used to having a certain window of time to do things in between. Just be aware and reduce the dough rest or prove times if needed by 15 to 30 minutes.

I usually reduce the length of any hand kneading instructions by a couple of minutes if using the mixer.

Proving doughs – this can be one of the hardest things to learn to gauge. Get used to training your eye to see if it is roughly double the size. If you've put it in a clear bowl, you can lift it up and see the bubbles that have puffed up underneath and at the sides.

Watching many baking shows can make you feel like there is this optimum window for the dough to be perfect and that is true to some extent, but your bake will still be delicious if it isn't perfectly proved. As long as it's had some chance to prove and is cooked through.

Tepid water

Tepid water, it annoys me that term, but I still use it because the options are limited! Tepid, room temperature and words like these describe the temperature of the water. I did not find these enough for me as I learned to mix bread and other doughs. But I still use them in recipes here because I want you to be able to transfer the skills you learn. When I specify 'tepid water', I use a small amount of freshly boiled kettle water and then add cold tap water. Once it's roughly the same temperature as your finger, when you dip it in, then you're there. If not, then add a little more boiled water, or cold water, depending on how warm or cold it felt. Where it's needed, I've given guidance on how I get a temperature of water that I like to work with for certain recipes. I hope it helps your dough making easier to carry out.

Weighing water

Why have I given you most of the liquid measurements in grams? Because I have learned weighing water is more accurate. When we use our eyes to judge the millilitres of liquids, the amount can vary. Jugs are, however, handy for pouring the wet mixtures into the dry ingredients. Your baking will be even more improved by weighing your liquids.

Spraying steam for sourdough baking

On each sourdough recipe I give the option for using a clean water sprayer when baking. I haven't added this into the instructions because you need to check your oven suitability for this. If you are able to try it, spray it on the inside of the oven and not the bread. Do this once you have placed both the loaves for baking and the tin of boiling water safely in the oven. Then quickly close the oven door. It really did help my sourdough loaves to open up more in baking, in a home oven. Some home ovens also have steam options.

Oven temperatures

Adjust your oven slightly if you need to. You know your oven. If it is a little on the hot side or cool side usually, then adjust the temperature slightly.

Egg substitutes

I mention egg substitute in some recipes for a plant-based option. And there are many of these that you can try out yourself. For example, mixing 1 tablespoon of ground flaxseed or ground chia mixed with 3 tablespoons of water is equal to one medium egg. You can readily buy liquid egg substitute in a carton that is of the aquafaba variety. 3 tablespoons of this is enough for 1 medium egg. If you're baking something cake-like, then pureed cooked fruit can be a good substitute. 45 grams of apple puree is equivalent to 1 medium egg. It may take some tinkering to get it to your desired consistency but many plant options are available to try and add deliciousness to your baking.

Butter and plant butter

Keep it simple here. If the recipe calls for butter or plant butter then use the block variety. Spreads made with butter, margarine or plant butter have a different consistency and will not give the same result. The bake may even flop because of the extra oil and water content in it. I give reminders in the recipes to help avoid this common pitfall.

Flour

If you can, use organic flour varieties. They are pesticide free and kinder to our environment. In my opinion, the flavour and quality of bread we make from it is better.

Reducing single-use items

Silicone baking liners are great instead of greaseproof paper. These can be cut to size and used time and time again. Find them online or in local baking shops. Buy a large wax wrap or shower cap that will fit the large width of a bowl to prove the dough.

You can add a little oil to the underside if you worry about it reaching the top and touching the wrap or shower cap. This stops the dough sticking to the top. These can be reused.

Fed starter

When I refer to 'fed starter' in my recipes, this refers either to a premade starter you have bought, or the starter recipe I provide on page 19. A fed starter is one that has been fed with strong flour and water 12 hours before mixing the sourdough ingredients (though I have a shorter solution for you on page 39 if you need it).

Sourdough storage

I find a sourdough loaf should last for up to 6 days at normal room temperature. This is amazing as it has no added preservatives doing this and it shows they aren't needed. So here is my list of storage answers for sourdough I've gathered so far.

- Wrap it in wax wrap or cling film and put it in a cool place

- Place it sliced side down in your bread bin

- Put it in a clean linen or cotton bag

- For long-term storage put it in a reusable freezer bag or wrapped tightly in cling film and place it in the freezer for up to a month

- Slice it, then wrap it as a loaf in a reusable freezer bag or cling film, place it in the freezer and take a slice out as you need it

To defrost a whole loaf, you can put it in a preheated oven at 150°C fan/170°C/gas 3 for 20-30 minutes until the loaf is soft and fully thawed in the middle – adapt this as you go as different ovens may take different times. You may find wrapping it in foil first helps to retain the texture you like.

To defrost slices for toasting, you can put a frozen slice straight under the grill or in the toaster. Or you can put slices on a baking sheet or tray, then cover with a little foil for about 5-10 minutes at 150°C fan/170°C or gas 3, if you want it untoasted.

If you have a microwave, you can also make use of that. For a large loaf try it on the defrost setting, unwrapped for 6 minutes and then check it at regular intervals until fully defrosted.

Many customers I have spoken to, who like to make or buy a large loaf for a small household, often cut the loaf in half and then freeze one half. Or they slice half a loaf and freeze it for getting one slice out at a time. A gentleman was waiting for my delivery when I arrived at the farm shop. He told me he liked to buy one large classic sourdough loaf, slice it all and then freeze it, and it lasted him all week.

Often, I'll make a couple of loaves for the family and get one out from the freezer the night before and leave it wrapped on the kitchen worktop. Ready for the morning rush.

> And one of my favourite things to do, if I've had a flurry of baking, is to gift loaves to others.

Utensils

My aim for these recipes is to equip home bakers with recipes that could be started straight away, without the need for investing in expensive equipment. After all, that's how my bread baking business began. A mixing bowl, wooden spoon, measuring scales, jug and a tea towel covers most making. And I used to bake 2 sourdoughs at a time in my home oven, where all I needed was a heavy baking sheet, some oven gloves and a small roasting dish. Start with what you have, it's rewarding bringing life to your creations with the bare minimum. And it's a more sustainable way to start.

Each recipe in the book will use most of the following utensils. I will also list additional utensils for that particular recipe.

Utensils that most recipes will need:

- 2 large mixing bowls

- Wooden spoon

- Optional - Electric hand mixer or free-standing mixer with dough hook/s and large bowl

- Digital scales

- Measuring jug

- Clean shower cap, wax wrap or cling film

- Space in a warm airing cupboard or an oven with only the light on (for proving in cold weather)

- Dough scraper, dough divider or a wide bladed knife

- Clean tea towel

- Kettle

- Oven – fan, conventional or gas

- Oven gloves

- Cooling rack or you can even use the inside rack taken from an oven grill

- Optional - Banneton basket. These are small containers made from rattan or wood pulp. Many come with a cotton liner, which is handy for sticky dough and when making flavoured sourdoughs. Different sizes are available. 22cm diameter is good for a round 900g loaf. The 21cm long oval ones are good for the half-size sourdough of 450g. But if you're a few centimetres different it won't affect it too much. If you want a wider, flatter loaf, go for a a wider banneton. Glass or plastic bowls lined with a clean tea towel are just as good to use.

- Water sprayer – see 'My Baking Tips' on page 11 for more details

- Silicone baking tray liners – these are reusable and reduce the need for greaseproof paper

- Baking tray or baking sheet – a sheet is usually more of a square shape and a tray is rectangular. Either is fine.

Baking Motivation

Dear reader,

Sometimes we give up on a recipe before we've even tried. I think you'll understand what I mean. We read through the recipe and think, Oh no I can't do it, I don't have this ingredient and that piece of equipment. And we talk ourselves out of it. Just a trace of motivation is needed here to make the start. Get the missing ingredients and borrow equipment from a friend or neighbour, at the next opportunity. This action will help you begin. And it is making a start that can be the hurdle between baking and not baking. Seems obvious, but it is part of the process to change our habits. And not just with baking.

Then we can often find we've been side-tracked by our responsibilities, or we've ended up doing the whole food shop for the week, when we all we meant to do was buy ingredients for our enticing recipe. That's life, isn't it? By the time we get home, we're thinking we'll give up on the whole baking idea for today. Or we've plain forgotten about it. Please don't leave it there. If you're a serial recipe watcher and reader, only to lose the interest to make, please use what you've done so far. Plan it into your week. Literally put it on your calendar. This is time you are making for you to do something enjoyable and to make breads without all the additives we don't need.

Equally, the same demotivation can happen when reading a recipe. We have the ingredients needed, read through the recipe and decide that it's just too complicated. I've been there and still do this at times.

It can seem overwhelming and I see this as the reason for many people to choose to opt out of baking bread.

You have a choice here. Choose another recipe that looks simpler for now or choose to view the stages of the recipe as just that. Focus on one part at time. Do the first steps. Then, if there's a stage of dough resting, don't wait around. Set a timer and use that time to do something else in between. This is where we learn to fit recipes into our day. The kind of things I've done with this between time are business admin, gardening, childcare, household duties, outings, exercise and meditation. This is where we can choose to bring baking into our lives to create a calmer wellbeing and an achievable skill that works around our life.

I've discovered this makes it more interesting for your brain and it gradually grows your ability and confidence to attempt more diverse recipes. By doing this, the food world you explore grows and so does the choice of food you bake in your home. What can be more amazing than that? Baking and cooking from scratch. As a bonus, saving you money and reducing the number of additives going into your mouth. A gift of free, sustainable skills for life. Hopefully, you will use these skills more and more and share with others in your life.

> You can do it; you will become more resilient and you will grow. What if it turns out to be something you never knew you could enjoy so much?

Sourdough Recipes

Sourdough Starter

A sourdough starter is what is often described as a 'wild yeast'.
It is a different yeast to the fast action ones used in many recipes.
It is made from strong bread flour and water. We allow the naturally
existing yeasts in the flour and the air to go into it, by leaving the lid
off. WHAT? I hear you say. What are these things we cannot see?
I know! Once you get over the surprise or even the alarming feeling
from this fact, you can marvel at the thought that you can make bread
from wild and free yeast. Sustainable or what? And with this starter,
we store it and then feed it from time to time. It can be your pet
if you so choose, but feeding it every day, once it's matured, isn't
compulsory. I feed mine twice a week as standard. Then more if I'm
doing more baking days. I use my starters to bake sourdough loaves,
pizza, focaccia, cookies and so much more. My pet starters are
Gordon the Mature White Flour, The 3 Vs, The Mature Rye Starter
and Wilf the Adolescent Wholemeal. I am also proud that one of my
lockdown delivery customers recently made one and named hers
after me. Thanks, Frances!

Ingredients

- 600g–900g strong bread flour of your
  choice: dark rye, white or wholemeal.
  It's best to use one flour and stick with
  it. You can make more than one starter
  at a time if you want a different bread
  flour in each one.

- Room temperature water (for the
  amounts see the method on the
  next page').

Extra Utensils

- A 1 litre clean Tupperware box
  with tight fitting lid.

See the section 'The Sourdough
Clean-Up' on page 7 for my tips on
how to dispose of excess starter and
clean your utensils.

Method

Read this recipe through before you start, to get a feel for it.

Starter day 1

Mix 200g of your bread flour with 200g of tepid water in the mixing bowl, until no lumps remain. Pour or spoon it into your chosen box. Keep the lid **off** and put it somewhere warm overnight, which will depend on the time of year. An airing cupboard is often good in the winter. A warm kitchen in the late spring or summer will be fine.

Starter day 2

Get the pot with your starter in. Throw away about half of your starter – I know it seems brutal, but you will just end up with too much. Add 100g of tepid water and 100g of your bread flour and mix it with a wooden spoon until incorporated. Leave the lid **off** and return it to somewhere warm again.

Starter day 3

Repeat all of the processes you did on **starter day** 2, including discarding half of the starter first.

Starter days 4, 5 and 6

Your mixture is taking in natural yeasts from the air. It will gradually start to be living in a lively way. If things aren't happening as quickly as you'd like, keep trying and have faith that things will happen for your starter.

For days 4, 5 and 6 – repeat the full process of **starter day** 2.

What you will begin to see are bubbles in the flour and water mixture. Once you get these bubbles you are creating a live, natural yeast! You are creating something from seemingly nothing! You are ready to make your first sourdough recipe. How amazing is that? The longer you keep using this starter, the more it will mature and the better your loaves and bakes will become.

The next step, once you have lots of bubbles and you are ready to make your loaf, is to weigh out the starter amount needed for your recipe. You can then keep the rest of your starter in your box and place it in the fridge. Before feeding the starter for your recipe, you will need to bring your starter out of the fridge and let it sit at room temperature for a couple of hours. Then feed it for the recipe, usually the night before making the dough. A starter that is new will bake very differently to a starter that is at least 6 months old or older. But both will turn out loaves with good results.

If you are not ready to make a sourdough recipe yet, put the lid on your container, put it in the fridge and feed it at least once a week, as described below. People baking every day don't need to refrigerate their starters as it is in a constant cycle of feeding and usage.

Keeping your starter alive

Feeding your starter once a week will mean that it is lively and ready to be put to use. I often feed the starter by bringing it to room temperature the evening before I am due to make a sourdough. I then feed it using the steps below. I often then leave it out overnight and then it is lively and ready to use the following morning for baking.

Feeding your starter

1. Get the starter out of the fridge at around 5pm and leave it on your kitchen counter with the lid **on** this time for about 2 hours.

2. Feed the starter by repeating the process of **starter day 2** on page 21. Put the lid back **on** the container.

3. Leave the starter on the counter until you come to use it the next morning. In the morning weigh the amount of starter needed for your recipe. Put the rest back in the fridge with the lid **on**, remembering to feed it once a week.

Troubleshooting

If your starter amount is getting too big for the container you can either discard some or you can get a bigger container to put it in.

It's okay if the starter smells strong and gluey, this is the natural yeast doing its thing.

It's okay if the starter has a greyish layer on the top. This is called 'hooch'. You can pour it off or stir it in. Leaving it in adds to the sourness, if you enjoy that.

You can use various types of flour for a starter. Wholemeal, dark rye and white bread flours are popular ones to use. I would recommend using one flour type in one starter.

Don't be scared of making mistakes and don't be put off if it feels like it isn't working. I made lots of mistakes and it's where we truly learn about how to bring the starter to a workable state.

Don't be tempted to throw away your starter if it feels like it isn't going right. Keep persevering with it. You can always start another one off. Some people have many different types of starters in their possession. Unless there are signs of an unusual mould or pink bacteria then you can continue safely with yours.

I'm going on holiday, do I need to take my starter? I don't, but some people may show that they do. If I go away for up to 2 weeks, I will place the starter in the fridge and feed it well for a few days when I return.

> Don't worry and just have fun with it. It's a chemical experiment!

Classic White Sourdough

Beginner to Intermediate

Here is a refined version of the first sourdough recipe I ever
perfected. It has always been a favourite with customers, who
love it for toasties, butties and even sliced very thinly for canapés.

It's the first loaf I entered for an award and it won a Gold medal
at the Free From Food Awards in 2023, in the tree nut and peanut free
category. An absolute highlight of my baking career: a win for those
with food allergies and confirmation that it was a tasty sourdough,
irrespective of what it stood for. Make it and you'll soon find out why.
The rye or wholemeal starter makes it easier to handle. Your final
loaves will be a white flour loaf with great texture from the starter.

This makes 2 x 900g baked loaves

Ingredients

- 680g tepid water*

- 200g fed starter of a rye or
  wholemeal flour starter

- 1kg white bread flour

- 25g table salt or salt flakes

Extra Utensils

- Optional - water sprayer

- Room in the fridge for your 2
  doughs overnight

*Make this water, depending on the season's temperatures, by choosing one of
these options: In a winter kitchen, I weigh up 100g boiled water with 580g cold tap
water in a jug. In spring and autumn, I use 50g of boiled and then add 630g of
cold tap water. In summer heat, I just weigh 680g of cold tap water.

Method

1. Place the weighed water into a large mixing bowl.

2. Add the weighed starter to the water and mix gently with a wooden spoon or comfortable mixing utensil.

3. Add the weighed flour to the water and starter, then mix with your hands or your utensil until it is a rough looking dough.

4. Now leave the dough uncovered in the bowl on the worktop for 45 minutes. After 45 minutes, mix in the salt with your hands or wooden spoon and cover the bowl with a tea towel.

5. You can skip step 4 if you are short on time and simply mix the salt in and cover with a tea towel.

You will need to follow the method, resting, folding, shaping and baking instructions from these pages (25 to 28) for the other sourdough recipes on pages 29 to 40.

Resting & Folding

How you rest and fold the dough can be flexible to fit around your day. I know that sounds a bit daunting, if you like structure to this baking routine, but I want to reassure you that you will get a great sourdough loaf, whichever way you choose. Low maintenance dough making has been this way since bread began.

If you are going to be away from the sourdough all day, that's fine. Before you go out, fold the sourdough 12 times, using the instructions below.

If you will be around the sourdough for the day, fold it at 3 separate times. One now, then in 3 hours' time, then finally 1 hour after that, as per the instructions below. Use a timer to remind you.

To Fold

1. Use a clean hand or use a suitable food safe glove.

2. Keep the dough in the bowl.

3. Grab a part of the dough from underneath, pull it upwards and outwards, and fold it onto the dough, into the top centre of the dough mass.

4. Gently fold it: **don't push it down**. This is to encourage more air bubbles.

5. Rotate the bowl as you do this action 12 times in total.

6. Return the tea towel over the bowl.

Timings are very flexible, so do feel free to change it to suit you and your day. In my experience, I would keep to the total fold and rest time, where possible (approximately 4 hours and 45 minutes to 5 hours), especially in the summer when the sourdough mass is a lot quicker to ferment and therefore break down.

First Shaping

After the resting and folding stage, you are ready to turn the dough out and shape into a boule.

1. First, use some additional white bread flour to dust the work surface. Turn your dough out, with the top of the dough positioned face down on the worktop.

2. Divide your dough into 2 by cutting it in half with a wide knife or dough scraper and shape each loaf by working on one at a time. To bring the dough back to a round shape after cutting, cup the sides of the dough, go around the edge with your cupped hands and pull down ever so gently. The result will be tucking

the underneath in as the top stretches slightly. Avoid tearing the outside dough layer as this helps form your sourdough crust.

3. Repeat with the second dough.

4. Rest both loaves on the floured work surface, leaving a gap in between them for growth. Sprinkle each with a little bread flour. Cover each with a tea towel and leave to rest for 45 minutes to 1 hour in winter, spring and autumn. 30 minutes in summer.

Final Shaping

1. Line 2 clean medium bowls with clean tea towels and flour them well. Or sprinkle each banneton well with white bread flour. Dust the work surface with flour. Turn your dough upside down onto the flour, using the dough scraper if you have one, or your hand. The wetter side is facing upwards. Be gentle with your dough, so all the gas you have worked hard to keep, remains in there. Let it open out a little and spread. Pick up the bottom edge and fold it into the middle. Then take each of the side flaps and fold them into the middle like an envelope. Then pull the remaining top flap down over the bottom and side flaps, that you have just folded in the dough.

2. At this point you can now move to step 3. Or you can choose to add extra structure to the dough, by what I describe as 'overlapping'. This is the gathering of opposite pieces of the face up dough together and then overlapping them as you move along the dough length. You can leave this step out. If you do want to overlap, you take hold of a little of the dough at the right end – one at the top and one nearest to you. Now pull those inwards and cross them over slightly. They may stick well or they may need a slight bit of pressure to stick. Do this from right to left, one at a time, until you reach the end.

3. Now use your dough scraper or your hand to lift the dough up and place it gently into the bowl or basket, messy side facing up. The smoother side will be touching the tea towel or banneton. You may even see some large bubbles and that's great. Repeat steps 1, 2 (optional) and 3 with the second dough.

Final shaping in action for step 2.

Final Rest

Place the bowls in the fridge and leave them uncovered overnight to rest and prove. A slower fermentation will give you a successful loaf that has had chance to develop fully.

Baking Day Utensils

- Thick baking sheet or a baking stone or pizza stone
- Steep sided roasting tin
- Very sharp knife or bread lame
- 2 x thin wooden boards
- Pastry brush

Method

1. *Take your loaves out of the fridge. They will rest while the oven heats. Preheat the oven to 230°C fan/250°C (or 240°C if it goes no higher) /gas 8. Put your baking sheet or baking / pizza stone on the middle shelf of the oven. Place your empty roasting tin on the bottom shelf of the oven while it preheats. Fill the kettle with water and boil.

2. When the oven has reached temperature turn your loaf out, smooth side up, onto a floured thin wooden board. Dust the excess flour off the top and sides of the loaf with the pastry brush. Use a very sharp knife or bread lame to cut one long line from the top of the round to the bottom of the round nearest you. This shouldn't be too deep, but deep enough so the top skin slightly opens and you see the stickier dough underneath. Hopefully you will see a few gluten strands.

3. Scoring for the classic: 1 straight score down the right-hand side and a wheat sheaf gently scored on the left-hand side.

4. Have your boiled kettle full of water next to your oven. Open the oven door and slide your loaf from your wooden board onto your baking sheet / stone. Immediately and safely pour the kettle of boiled water into the roasting tin below. Be careful of boiling steam rising up. Shut the oven door as soon as you can. Bake for 15 minutes.

5. After 15 minutes turn the oven down to 190°C fan/210°C/gas 6 and bake for another 30 minutes. When finished, remove the loaves from the oven and allow them to cool fully on a wire rack.

* You can bake both loaves together if you can fit them side by side or diagonally in your oven. If you do cook them at the same time, prepare them for the oven on 2 separate boards. It makes shuffling them into the oven much easier. Or you can leave your second loaf in the fridge in its basket / bowl, while the first one bakes. Once the first one has finished, empty the roasting tin of water. Preheat the oven again to 230°C fan/250°C/gas 8 and boil the kettle. Remove the second loaf from the fridge to rest while it preheats. Repeat exactly as for the first loaf with the boiling water etc. Once fully cooled this will keep for up to 6 days. They freeze and defrost so well. It's a lovely way to prolong the gift to yourself after all your hard work spent making it.

'70/30' Wholemeal & White Sourdough

Beginner to Intermediate

I love the delicious flavour of this loaf. It has 700g of wholemeal
and 300g of white. I blend it like this to retain a springy texture to
the cooked sourdough. It really is one of my favourites and goes
with absolutely everything.

This makes 2 x 900g baked loaves

Ingredients

- 750g tepid water*

- 200g fed starter of a rye or white
  flour starter. I find a rye or wholemeal
  starter works really well for handling
  and for puffier texture.

- 300g white bread flour

- 700g wholemeal bread flour

- 25g table salt or salt flakes

Extra Utensils

- Optional - water sprayer

- Room in the fridge for your 2
  doughs overnight

*Make this water, depending on the season's temperatures, by choosing one of these
options: In a winter kitchen, I weigh 100g boiled water with 650g cold tap water in a
jug. In spring and autumn, I use 50g of boiled water and then add 700g
of cold tap water. In summer heat, I just weigh 750g of cold tap water.

Method, resting, folding & baking

Follow the instructions from page 25.

The only difference is the way I like to score
the 70/30: 1 straight score down middle.

Deep Malthouse Sourdough

Beginner to Intermediate

I thought the classic was a popular one, but when I blended it with malthouse flour from Shipton Mill, this soon became a searched for item from my customers. It comes out like a puffy granary style loaf. It's great for people who don't eat nuts or seeds because the fermented grain in the malthouse flour gives it a lovely texture. I hope you enjoy it.

This makes 2 x 900g baked loaves

Ingredients

- 695g tepid water*

- 200g fed starter of a rye or white flour starter. I find a half and half starter works really well for handling and for puffier texture.

- 800g white bread flour

- 200g malthouse grain flour

- 25g table salt or salt flakes

Extra Utensils

- Optional - water sprayer

- Room in the fridge for your 2 doughs overnight

*Make this water, depending on the season's temperatures, by choosing one of these options: In a winter kitchen, I weigh up 100g of boiled water with 595g cold tap water in a jug. In spring and autumn, I use 50g of boiled water and then add 645g of cold tap water. In summer heat, I just weigh 695g of cold tap water.

Method, resting, folding & baking

Follow the instructions from page 25.

The only difference is the way I like to score the deep malthouse: 1 straight score down the middle or try a circle score around the top. It lifts up when baking sometimes, like it's tipping its hat to you!

Chef's Rye Blend Sourdough

Beginner to Intermediate

My chef's rye is so called because it's one I made regularly for a Michelin trained private chef. He ordered it week after week, along with other bakes. It worked very well for a bread basket and for morning toast. It's a mix of the classic with a proportion of the dark rye flour. For a dark rye tin loaf, see page 75.

This makes 2 x 900g baked loaves

Ingredients

- 700g tepid water*

- 200g fed starter of a rye or wholemeal flour starter.

- 800g white bread flour

- 200g dark rye bread flour

- 25g table salt or salt flakes

Extra Utensils

- Optional - water sprayer

- Room in the fridge for your 2 doughs overnight

*Make this water, depending on the season's temperatures, by choosing one of these options: In a winter kitchen, I weigh 100g of boiled water with 600g of cold tap water in a jug. In spring and autumn, I use 50g of boiled water and then add 650g of cold tap water. In summer heat, I just weigh 700g of cold tap water.

Method, resting, folding & baking

Follow the instructions from page 25.

The only difference is the way I like to score the chef's rye: 1 straight score down the middle and then another straight score down the middle at the cross section.

Flavoured Sourdoughs

There are so many ways you can go with flavoured sourdough.
There are lots of lightbulb ideas of flavours I've tried out. Here, I
include the ones that my family and customers go back to time and
time again. If you have an idea for a flavour combination, then go
for it. The experiment could result in the next best thing.

I've provided the flavouring amounts, where in the recipe to
add them, plus extra information of which flour blend to use,
where I believe it makes a difference. Otherwise, you can use
the flour choices of the sourdough type you prefer.

Some flavours add moisture to the mixture, e.g. jalapeños in brine.
I've refined the water content in the recipe to allow for this.
Wholemeal and rye flours soak up a lot more water than white
flour, so it's always good to remember this. And salt levels in some
ingredients mean I've adjusted the salt added to the recipe.
Always line your bannetons, if using them, with a fabric liner or clean
tea towel, to protect them from strong flavours and food debris.
The liners can then be washed with unperfumed laundry liquid.

Where possible, rest your flavour ingredients at room temperature
before adding.

Follow the instructions from page 25, along with the pointers on
the next page.

Apricot & Cinnamon

This makes 2 large loaves

Ingredients

- 700g tepid water
- 4 tsp ground cinnamon – add at the water stage
- 200g fed starter
- 900g white flour
- 100g wholemeal flour
- 20g table salt
- 150g dried apricots, chopped into 1cm chunks – fold in at the final fold stage or 1 hour before you turn out the dough for a final rest

Jalapeño Pepper & Cheese

Makes 2 large loaves

Ingredients

- 690g tepid water
- 222g fed starter
- 900g white flour
- 100g wholemeal flour
- 20g salt
- 200g grated extra strong Cheddar or another strong cheese of similar consistency
- 120g well drained jalapeños from a jar, roughly chopped with a few left whole – fold both in at the final fold stage or 1 hour before you turn out the dough for a final rest.

Honey & Oat

Makes 2 large loaves

Ingredients

- 700g tepid water
- 3 tbsp honey or agave syrup for a vegan option – add at the water adding stage
- 200g starter
- 700g white flour
- 200g wholemeal flour
- 100g rolled oats – add at the flour stage
- 20g salt

- A handful of jumbo or rolled oats for topping. Soak in cold water for 10 minutes and drain and place on a baking tray or sheet. Use a liner to put in the bannetons or a tea towel liner in a bowl or the oats can get stuck to your overnight proving vessel. It's a little fiddly here. Dip the outer side of the sourdough into the oats before placing in the overnight vessel. Or try and coat the lined vessel with the oats before placing the sourdough in.

Marmite & Vintage Cheddar

Makes 2 large loaves

Ingredients

- 100g recently boiled tap water with 60g Marmite mixed well into it – once mixed, add to the sourdough mixing bowl after adding the 530g cold water for the recipe first

- 530g cold tap water – add to the mixing bowl first

- 200g fed starter

- 800g white flour

- 150g wholemeal flour

- 16g salt

- 200g grated vintage style Cheddar or another strong cheese of similar consistency - fold in at the final fold stage or 1 hour before you turn out the dough for a final rest.

The Vegan & Free From Savoury

Makes 2 large loaves

Ingredients

Use the ingredients guide for the previous loaf and replace:

- Marmite with a yeast extract that does not contain celery. This is available in many stores.

- Cheddar with a vegan type of cheddar. I like to use the Cathedral City plant based range as I've found that to be the most similar in flavour and it does not contain tree nuts.

I created this loaf for the free from community, removing celery and tree nuts. Using Cathedral City plant based Cheddar means it's vegan too! This is most similar to the Marmite and vintage Cheddar. The top remaining allergens it contains are gluten (wheat and rye flours).

See You Later Sourdough

There are moments when you want to spend time making every step count for your sourdough. Other times you just want to get the loaf of sourdough done, so you can get on with life. Believe me, I know – and so many other people do too.

As you gain confidence with baking, you'll start to figure out how to use my sourdough recipe and make changes here and there where you can save time and speed things up.

Start with these guidelines I've made for you, in the hope it will encourage you to keep baking in busier times. I feel that's when we need good nourishment the most. Following these pointers will save you about half a day, or show you how you can fit in the prep and baking that best suits your timetable.

Let's say it's morning and you realise you want a loaf to get you through the week ahead. But it's a slow dough and you didn't feed it the night before: how do we feed it fast so we have a fed starter ASAP? We adapt how we do parts of the process. Use these pointers to make sourdough now, with less faff.

1. Prepare your starter for feeding as soon as you realise you want a loaf, using the amounts in the sourdough recipes.* If it's morning when you realise you want to make a loaf, you have time to get your sourdough starter from the fridge and allow it to sit at room temperature for an hour. However, if it's 1pm on a warm day and you want to make a loaf the next day, then you can save yourself a couple of hours by doing the feeding part without bringing the starter to room temperature (it's not ideal but it should still result in a successful loaf).

2. Whichever is your situation, once you've fed the starter you can then leave it on the counter with the lid on (on a hot day, leave in a place out of the heat).

3. At around 8pm that same day, hopefully most of the demands of the day have abated and you have time for the next steps. Use your starter and ingredients list from any of my unflavoured sourdough recipes in this book to mix your desired sourdough and add the salt before mixing too.

4. Before going to bed, do the 12 folds (step 5, page 26) and cover the sourdough, in the bowl, with a clean tea towel. Leave in a cool room overnight.

5. The next morning, head to the kitchen and spend 5 minutes turning out, dividing and doing the first shaping of your sourdough (see page 26) before allowing it to rest for 30 minutes, on the worktop at room temperature, with a tea towel draped over it.

6. Get ready for your day ahead.

7. After your sourdough has rested for 30 minutes, do the second shape (the 'envelope' shaping, page 27) before putting the sourdough into your floured bannetons or bowls, each lined with a clean tea towel. Pop them in the fridge and get on with your day.

8. You then have a choice of baking when you are available again, ideally over 8 hours later – something lovely to look forward to at the end of the day. Or bake the loaf or loaves the following morning, filling the house with the smell of delicious bread before you leave, or you may even be around to enjoy it as soon as it's cool enough to eat!

*Please refer to the recipe and baking instructions in the sourdough recipe of your choice in this recipe book, using the method on page 28. Some of the best sourdough results I've had have been achieved using this method. Maybe a lot can be learned from just doing less.

Sourdough Cobs

Beginner to Intermediate

Cobs, barm, bun, bap, roll, stotty. We all have our favourite name
for these, don't we? In Somerset, where I grew up, the word 'roll'
would encompass many things round and bready in our house.
In the Midlands, where I live at the moment, the word 'cob' is a term
of affection for baked little bread rounds you will be familiar with,
on the counter of a bar filled with the thickest slice of strong cheese
and sliced fresh onion. A cob by any other name, in any other town,
county or country would be just as great.

I have found on the day of baking that these cobs are a delightfully
crispy crusted roll with a softer centre. If kept in an airtight container,
the next day they have a slightly chewier crust. I think you'll find these
very satisfying. They go naturally with a soup or a slow cooked dinner.
Or try them filled with breakfast delights, or with the fillings you see
in cobs at the local pub.

This makes 10 cobs

Ingredients

- 465g room temperature water
  - mostly cold water with a dash of
  recently boiled water

- 135g fed and risen starter

- 700g strong white bread flour

- 4g ground salt

- Additional plain flour for rolling
  and dusting

Extra Utensils

- Small sharp knife

- Small high-sided tray for some boiling
  water in the oven

Method

1. Add the water and starter to the mixing bowl and mix gently.

2. Add the flour and salt and mix well until there are no floury bits left and the mixture isn't really runny.

3. Let the dough rest on the kitchen counter overnight with a shower cap, wax wrap or lightly oiled cling film over the bowl.

4. In the morning divide and shape the rolls. I like to weigh the dough amounts to roughly 122g per roll, but you can easily judge by eye for 10 similar sized rolls.

5. I keep the dough in the bowl and cut a piece off gently with a dough scraper – weigh it, if doing so, and add or take away dough to make 122g (approximately).

6. To shape the cob you can use your hand: claw it over the dough in a cupped shape and roll it around until the seam is underneath. Or you can use a dough scraper in one hand and your hand as a tool to turn it round and round as you push the dough scraper against the cob. Have loose plain flour on hand to help. Just avoid using too much.

7. Place the cob seam side down on a silicone sheet or greaseproof lined baking tray and leave a gap of about 2cm in between each cob, for each one to spread.

8. Repeat this until you have 10 cobs.

9. Sprinkle the cobs with plain flour and cover with a clean tea towel and leave to rise for 2 hours. If it's a really hot day this may be less. They should be doubled in size.

10. 30 minutes before the end of rising, preheat the oven to 210°C fan/230°C/gas 8.

11. Before placing them in the oven, remove the tea towel and score the cobs with a very sharp knife. Keep the depth of the scoring small: no further than ¼ depth into the cob. One quick movement diagonally across each is perfect.

12. Put the cobs in the hot oven and turn down the temperature to 190°C fan/210°C/Gas 6. You can place a small high-sided tray of boiling water on the rack underneath. This will help them to 'oven spring' more, but is not essential.

13. Bake for about 25 minutes, when they have risen and are looking golden brown. Halfway through cooking, you can turn the tray carefully so the back of the tray is now at the front of the oven. This helps get an even colour. Once risen and looking golden brown you can remove them after about 25 minutes.

Enjoy these in many different ways. For a simple vegan option, make a chip barm or butty. Simply spread the cob with vegan butter and add homecooked oven potato chips and your favourite sauce. Comforting!

Sourdough Pizza &
Homemade Pizza Sauce

Beginner to Intermediate

For this recipe you will need 135g of fed sourdough starter. For best results feed your starter the evening or morning before the day or evening you want to make your pizza dough. You can also make the dough the day before cooking and place it in the fridge in a bowl, covered tightly with wax wrap or cling film. Remove the bowl from the fridge 2 hours before use. This is a straightforward sourdough pizza recipe, but with a few challenges to help keep you learning. By an hour's time you will be well on your way to baking your homemade sourdough pizza. It will taste fantastic and you can add your favourite toppings, just the way you like it! The hardest part can be transferring the pizza into the oven, but don't worry, this recipe will cover that. It's helpful to read through the recipe first, before starting it.

Makes 2 x thin 10-inch pizzas or 1 x 10-inch deep pan pizza

Ingredients

- 135g fed and risen starter

- 465g room temperature water - mostly cold water with a dash of recently boiled water

- 700g strong white bread flour

- 4g ground salt

- Additional plain flour for rolling and dusting

Extra Utensils

- Small sharp knife

- Small high-sided tray for some boiling water in the oven

Ingredients - Pizza Sauce

- ½ tbsp olive oil

- 1 medium onion - finely chopped

- 1 clove of garlic - finely sliced

- ½ tsp salt

- 400g tin of chopped tomatoes

- 2 tsp fresh or dried chopped thyme

This recipe has been written so you can multitask with your dough making and pizza sauce recipe. If you prefer to make them separately, make the pizza sauce first and then make the dough afterwards.

Method

1. Weigh your sourdough starter amount into the mixing bowl. Add the warm water and mix gently with a wooden spoon. You can do this with a mixer and a dough hook, if you prefer. Add the flour and salt and mix to a rough texture with the wooden spoon.

2. Take the dough out of the bowl and start kneading. You shouldn't need to add much extra flour on the work surface. You can be quite rough with it. I lift it up in the air, smack it on the counter, stretch it out and repeat (quite therapeutic). Any way you like is fine, just make sure to stretch it out to get the gluten going. Alternatively, use the electric mixer and dough hook.

3. About 5 minutes of kneading is good – it's a little workout! If it sticks to the counter, use the side of a stiff spatula to scrape under the dough and get it off the counter. Put the dough back together. Just keep going. It will become less sticky and stretchier and smoother as you work it. In the electric mixer, mix for 3 minutes.

4. Place the dough back into the mixing bowl and use a clean tea towel to cover the bowl. Leave for 40-60 minutes. You can make this dough the day before and leave it in the bowl, covered tightly with cling film, overnight in the fridge instead.

Pizza Sauce

1. Time to make the pizza sauce. Heat the olive oil gently in a saucepan on a low heat. Add the onion, garlic and salt. Fry gently for about 5 minutes, until soft.

2. Stir the chopped tomatoes and thyme into the mixture. Cover the top of the mixture with a rough circle of greaseproof paper (or you can proudly call this a 'cartouche'). It traps in the flavours better than a regular lid. Simmer gently for 15 minutes.

3. Once the sauce has reduced, remove it from the heat. Add any salt and pepper that suits your taste buds. Allow the mixture to cool a little.

4. Puree the mixture using a stick blender or food processor. If you don't have a blender you can push the sauce through a sieve with a wooden spoon or use a potato masher. Keep enough sauce to top both pizzas. If you have any leftover you can keep it in the fridge for 5 days or freeze it for 2 months.

Back to the pizza dough

1. Preheat your oven to 210°C fan/230°C/gas 8. Place your baking sheet or pizza stone in to preheat too. If you have 2 baking sheets, place them both in the oven.

2. Now is your time to choose if you want the failsafe method of putting the pizzas in the oven or if you want the challenge of shuffling them in – warning, they may get misshapen, but it doesn't matter. Really, it doesn't.

3. For the failsafe method, cut 2 squares of greaseproof approximately the same shape as the baking sheet(s) or pizza

stone. Then flour them well. For the 'shuffle in method', flour 2 **wooden** chopping boards well. These are boards that will fit your finished pizza on, but won't go into the oven. The pizza dough will often stick to anything metal (lesson learned!)

4. Take your dough out of the bowl and cut it in half. Now make each into a ball. Place each ball of dough onto your squares of floured greaseproof or your wooden boards. Pull out the edges of the dough gently into a small circle of about 10cm across. Cover each loosely with a clean tea towel or cling film. Leave to rest for 5 minutes. During this time you can get the rest of your toppings ready.

5. After 5 minutes, remove the tea towel or cling film. You can now increase the size of your pizza. If you are worried it may tear, then leave this next part out and just stretch it on the greaseproof with your hands.

6. Otherwise, this is a moment to be brave and go for it! Make your hand into a fist. Place one of the dough circles on top of your fist. Gently circle your fist so the dough spins around it and you will find the dough stretches quite quickly. Be careful not to let it tear. You can guide it with your other hand as it increases in size. Aim for about 20-25cm diameter. This is an attempt at 'throwing' a pizza!

7. Place the pizza back on the floured greaseproof or wooden board and do the same with the other one. If it does tear, don't worry. Seal the hole with a bit of dough pushed into it. If it isn't a perfect circle that is perfectly okay. We want the flavour to be the hero.

8. It's time to add your homemade pizza sauce. 2 tablespoons on each pizza should be about right. Follow this with mozzarella, Cheddar, or other cheeses. Use vegan cheese here if you like. Then add your chosen toppings. Be careful not to overload it, in case it makes it soggy.

9. I'm not going to sugar-coat this, the next part of getting the pizza into the oven can be tricky. But it will be worth it. If you have your pizzas on greaseproof paper, put your oven gloves on and open the oven door ready. Then carefully shuffle one pizza, including the greaseproof paper, onto the baking sheet. Shut the oven door.

10. For the wooden boards, open the oven door. Using oven gloves, carefully pull the baking sheet or pizza stone slightly forward. Then pick up your wooden board with the pizza on and place the edge of the board near the back of the pizza stone or baking sheet. Give the board a hard shove towards the sheet or stone. Keep doing this until the pizza shuffles onto the baking sheet or stone. If it is untidy or even looks catastrophic, don't worry. It will still rise up, bake and taste great.

11. Bake for about 15-20 minutes or until the dough is cooked through to the middle and the cheese is golden brown. Reduce the oven to 180°C fan/200°C/ gas 6 if it is browning too much. If you are baking one at a time, put your next pizza in.

Enjoy your pizza as it is, or add more fresh herbs, black pepper, dried chilli flakes, or extra virgin olive oil. Take a photo of your hard work, then slice it up. Enjoy every bite, while thinking of the next topping masterpiece!

Sourdough Focaccia

Intermediate

Sourdough focaccia is definitely more satisfying in terms of beating hunger. It gives more thickness of dough and the bubbles develop as it bakes. When feeding your starter for this, try and make it a fairly stiff starter, as it helps with the texture. This dough is made and then put in the fridge overnight before baking. Start it late afternoon or evening, when you have 3 hours for the resting and making. The toppings you add bring your own style of what you enjoy, and you can introduce them to others. One of my favourites is artichoke hearts, roasted pepper, pink onions and rosemary running through it. A vegan snack that will last you well or use it as a base for a melted cheese topping or pizza. You decide what you like and you're away.

This makes 1 focaccia (20cm x 30cm)

Ingredients

- 400g room temperature water (mostly cold water with a dash of recently boiled water)

- 550g strong white bread flour

- 150g fed and risen starter

- 30g room temperature water - mostly cold water with a dash of recently boiled water

- 15g flaked or table salt

- 45g olive oil

- Optional topping ideas at room temperature – rosemary, sea salt, roasted pepper, cooked onions, artichoke hearts prepared to your liking

Extra Utensils

- Medium rectangular, square or circular baking pan or tray, lined with greaseproof paper

Tip: Be careful that any toppings you add are not likely to burn during baking e.g. tomato based sauce or cheese. These would need to be added and grilled **after** the focaccia is baked.

Method

1. Place the flour and water in the bowl and mix to a rough dough by hand or with a wooden spoon and then leave to rest in the bowl, uncovered, for 45 minutes.

2. After resting your dough, mix in the starter, gradually adding the 30g of room temperature water as you go. Then add the salt and mix again.

3. Let the dough rest again on the kitchen counter for 1 hour with a tea towel draped over the bowl. On a cooler day you may need to put this somewhere warm.

4. After an hour, stretch and fold the dough in the bowl. Use your hand to grab part of the round dough, stretch it upwards and place it back into the centre of the dough. Continue in a clockwise direction roughly 10 times. Keep the dough in the bowl and cover with the tea towel and leave to rest again for another hour.

5. After the second hour, use your hands to rub some of the olive oil onto the greaseproof in the bottom of the baking pan. Then use a dough scraper or spatula to transfer the dough from the bowl to the pan and gently ease it out towards the corners of your pan. It will have a chance to grow again, out towards the edges so don't worry that you need to stretch it.

6. Add some of the oil to the top of the focaccia dough and very gently rub it evenly over the top. This helps to create a seal to the dough so it won't form a skin. Keep the rest for the morning.

7. Place in a fridge overnight for about 12-18 hours, uncovered. I sometimes put the baking pan I'm using inside another one, in case the oil escapes over the top of the pan.

8. In the morning, take it out of the fridge and leave it to sit somewhere warm for about 3 hours (maybe less on a warm day). You want it to be at least room temperature and with signs of the bubbles appearing.

9. 15 minutes before the end of this 3-hour rest period, preheat the oven to 200°C fan/220°C/gas 7.

10. Before placing it in the oven, add your chosen toppings. Be careful not to overload and also make sure the toppings are at room temperature. For a classic focaccia, use fresh rosemary and a little flaked sea salt. Add the remaining olive oil.

11. Then push your fingertips down into the focaccia to make dimples all over the dough. Hopefully you will see some bubbles pop up as you do this.

12. Bake in the oven for 35-45 minutes. This is a thicker focaccia than my yeasted one, so it takes longer to cook. If it is getting too brown, gently place greaseproof paper or foil over it for the last 10-15 minutes. You can turn the temperature down towards the end if that helps to cook it for longer and through to the middle.

13. To check the middle, take the tray out of the oven and check carefully with an eating knife by poking in and pulling gently to the side to see if there is any raw in the middle. Place it back in the oven if it is still raw there and keep an eye on the oven temperature and colour of the bake as you finish it in the oven.

Allow to cool on a wire rack when finished. Then eat it as part of your meal spreads, picnics, snacks, pizzas, sandwiches or just have it warm from the oven. I dare you to resist.

Herby Sourdough Croutons

What can you do with any leftover sourdough bread?

We sometimes have 2 small ends left, which are the perfect
amount for using as croutons for your soup and salads. To make
the croutons you can choose to fry or bake them in the oven.
If you are on a lower fat diet then you can reduce the amount
of oil used or use the spray oil.

Method

1. Cut the sourdough ends into
   1cm chunks.

2. In a bowl, coat the sourdough with
   a tablespoon of oil and herbs of
   your choice.

3. I like to use fresh rosemary,
   finely chopped.

4. Bake in the oven on a preheated
   baking sheet or tray for 20 minutes
   at 160°C fan/180°C/gas 4 or fry on
   a medium heat until golden brown.

5. Remove from the oven or frying pan
   and sprinkle with salt and pepper to
   taste and allow to cool. Sprinkle on
   soup or salads. They will keep in
   an airtight container for 3 days in a
   cupboard if you're making them ahead.

Dough Recipes

First-Time Focaccia

Beginner

I call this first-time focaccia because it's a straightforward recipe
that you can try as one of your first bread bakes. I often use it when
showing budding bakers how to make their first recipe. It increases
confidence because it usually works out really well. Give it a try and
see if it makes you feel encouraged to bake more, as well as
enjoying the tasty end result.

Ingredients

- 300g strong white bread flour

- 7g fast action yeast

- 175g tepid water - 145g cold tap
  water and 30g of just boiled water

- 45g olive oil

- 1 tsp table salt

Topping

- 1 large sprig of rosemary – removed
  from the hard stalk

- 60g olive oil

- 1 tsp salt flakes

Extra Utensils

- Small bowl

- Heavy baking sheet or roasting tin
  (larger than 20cm x 25cm)

- Long ruler or tape measure

- Cling film or plastic proving bag

Method

1. In your large mixing bowl add the flour and yeast, then stir to combine.

2. Add the 175g of water and 45g of olive oil to the mixing bowl. Add the salt last and then mix with a wooden spoon or with the dough hook on an electric mixer. Mix for a couple of minutes until you have a shaggy dough.

3. Next you can knead the dough or you can continue with an electric mixer. For kneading by hand, add a little oil to your worktop and knead the sticky dough for 6 minutes. As you knead it, there may be a sticky stage before you come out the other side to a smooth, stretchy dough. You can use a dough scraper to gather any dough sticking to the worktop each time you knead. Just at the point where you feel it is never going to change, you will turn that corner, I promise. If using the electric mixer with the dough hook, do this on a medium speed for 5 minutes.

4. Put your dough into a lightly oiled bowl. Cover the bowl with a clean tea towel and leave it to prove for about 1 hour, until it has doubled in size. The time it takes will depend on the seasons. On a warm day an hour should be plenty with the bowl placed on the worktop. On a colder day it may take a little longer and will need the airing cupboard or in the oven with only the light switched on. If you're not sure about how to tell when it has doubled, take a photo of the dough when you first place it into the bowl. This should help you compare it.

5. While the dough is having its first prove, we can flavour the olive oil. Mix 60g of olive oil with the rosemary leaves in a small bowl. Then use a teaspoon to crush them against the side of the bowl a little just to release the flavour. Leave to stand.

6. After an hour, lightly grease your heavy baking sheet or roasting tin and line it well with greaseproof paper. The olive oil may seep out the sides once the focaccia has its topping, so allow for this by using enough greaseproof paper to capture it.

7. Take your dough out of the bowl and gently place it onto your baking sheet or in your tin. Stretch your dough with your hands to an even depth of 20cm x 25cm. And if the dough won't stretch any more, it will grow some more after the next prove.

8. Using your fingers, make little dips in your dough, but don't push right to the bottom. Drizzle your rosemary and olive oil all over the focaccia. It should puddle in the little dips. Sprinkle 1 tsp of salt flakes over the focaccia.

9. Cover the dough loosely with cling film or put the baking sheet or tin into a plastic proving bag and a clip on the end. Leave it to rise at room temperature for about 30-60 minutes. You are looking for it to have increased in size.

10. Towards the end of the second proving time, preheat your oven to 200°C fan/ 220°C/gas 7.

11. Place your baking sheet or tin containing your dough into the oven. Bake for 25 minutes or until a lovely golden colour.

12. When you take your focaccia out, place the tray or tin on a cooling rack.

Eat while still warm with your favourite accompanying dish or with a deli selection of olives, cheeses and meats. Focaccia, like most breads is at its very best the same day. But it can be wrapped or placed in a tin for up to 3 days. A little warming, if it goes a little solid, helps to soften it again. You can also wrap and freeze it for up to a month, as a whole focaccia or cut into squares.

Inspired Flatbreads

Beginner to Intermediate

I made these yeast free flatbreads a few times at home and they were very, very tasty, especially with the addition of melted cheese to their warm, enveloping wrap. Yum! I made a big batch and took them along to my market stall in Malvern one Sunday. One gentleman, running an Indian pop-up with dishes of the most delicious selection, came to see me before it got busy. His eyes were taken straight to these flatbreads. He said, 'These look tasty and they look like naan.'. He asked if he could try one out with his fillings, so I happily agreed. I was pleased it had created some interest and it brought me to this name of 'Inspired Flatbreads', because they take their inspiration from bread culture around the world, like Greek and Indian origin flatbreads.

These are fairly immediate, fun to make and really delicious. Try with a homemade dish that has lots of sauce to mop up or as a wrap with your filling creations. And you can always make them bigger if that's how you enjoy them too.

This makes between 6 and 8 flatbreads

Ingredients

- 210g plain flour (not strong bread flour) or gluten free white flour (you may need 230g for GF)

- ¾ tsp salt

- 50g unsalted butter or unsalted plant butter - melted

- 180g whole milk or plant milk – soya or oat work well

- Sunflower or other vegetable oil of your choice to grease the pan

Extra Utensils

- Optional - Electric hand mixer or free-standing mixer with dough hook/s and large bowl

- Rolling pin

- Non-stick frying pan or pancake pan, roughly 20cm wide

- Spatula

- Warm plate to place on afterwards

- Optional - Pastry brush

Method

1. In your mixing bowl or electric mixer bowl add the flour and salt and stir to combine.

2. Add the melted butter to your measured milk in a jug or small bowl and stir together briefly.

3. Add the wet ingredients to the dry and mix until combined. If it is very wet, you can add up to 30g of plain flour to get it to a consistency of being smooth, not flaky and not very wet.

4. Knead the dough on a floured work surface for about 3 minutes until it is smooth or in a stand mixer with a dough hook for 2 minutes. Place it in a lightly oiled bowl covered with a clean shower cap, wax wrap or cling film. Let it rest on the worktop for about 30-40 minutes.

5. Once rested, use a small amount of flour to lightly dust the worktop. Tip the dough out and divide into 6 or 8, depending on the size you are wanting.

6. Roll each one to about 20cm. Leave them on the worktop ready, as you fry each one in turn. You're headed for a circle shape or something resembling that. They are homemade so don't worry as each will be beautifully unique. Each flatbread should be a couple of millimetres thick.

7. To fry, grease your pan lightly with a little oil and wipe it round with a pastry brush or greaseproof paper. Heat the pan on the hob with a medium to high heat for a couple of minutes and then put your first flatbread in the pan for about 90 seconds. You can time this on your phone timer.

8. It will begin to puff (exciting!) and get golden or with slightly darker patches, which is fine. Then flip it on to the other side with a spatula. Let it cook for another minute, checking the colour as it cooks. Once ready it will puff a little again and be ready to put on the warm plate.

9. Continue to do this with each flatbread. Like a pancake pan gets hotter as you continue to use it, this will too. Turn down the heat a little if the flatbreads are getting too dark in a shorter time.

10. Place the flatbreads on top of each other on a warm plate as you go, if you are going to use them straight away. If not, you can pile them up on a board or plate and leave to cool. You may want to place greaseproof paper in between each one.

You can then serve straight away as an impressive side to a meal or a warming lunch wrap. Or let them cool and place them in an airtight container until you want to use them. They keep well for 3 days and can be reheated like a tortilla wrap in foil in the oven or on a plate for 10 seconds in the microwave. I see no reason why they couldn't be wrapped tightly and frozen for up to a month.

Brioche Burger Buns

Beginner to Intermediate

Burger buns! Great for a burger of any kind: veggie, vegan, meat,
fish, whatever you like. You can freeze these well wrapped for a
couple of weeks and use them for your barbecues. Warm them
gently before using them and they will feel lovely and fresh again.
I tried out many brioche burger bun recipes. Some were too
sweet and others were a bit too rigid. These ones are just the
right size for your burger creations and soft enough to get
in your mouth, if you've stacked it high. Keep a plain, shiny top
or add some onion seeds for a delicious flavour and texture.
Be careful not to overbake, that way you get a softer bun.

This makes 12 buns

Ingredients

- 600g strong white bread flour

- 6g fast action yeast

- 12g caster sugar

- 100g unsalted butter at room
  temperature or plant butter
  (not spread)

- 2 medium eggs or equivalent
  egg substitute

- 50g whole milk or plant milk
  – gently warmed but not hot

- 250g tepid water – 200g cold tap
  water with 50g boiling water

- 9g table salt

Glaze

- 1 egg (beaten) or sunflower / plant oil

- 1 tbsp onion seeds (optional)

Extra Utensils

- Whisk or fork

- Optional - Electric hand mixer or
  free-standing mixer with dough
  hook/s and large bowl

- 2 small bowls

- Pastry brush

Method

1. In your mixing bowl add the flour, yeast and caster sugar and mix together evenly.

2. Next add the butter and mix it using a paddle attachment with an electric mixer or with your hands to make it look like breadcrumbs. When doing by hand I like to pick up some mixture in each hand, face my hands towards me and push my thumb into each finger as I push the fingers into the thumb. As you do this it flattens and breaks down the lumps. Then collect more in your hands and keep repeating. Many of you will know this technique, but if you haven't tried it then it's a great skill to learn for pastry and is so therapeutic too.

3. Once there are no large lumps add the eggs, milk, water and salt and mix by hand, spoon or electric mixer with a dough hook until you have a rough dough.

4. Next, it's time to knead the dough. So, you can use the electric mixer with the dough hook for 5 minutes until smooth. Or you can do the stretch and fold on the worktop by hand. Give it a bash on the counter now and again too, it's good for an energy release! Use a small amount of flour on the work surface if kneading by hand.

5. When it's smooth and quite stretchy put the dough in a lightly oiled bowl and cover it with cling film, wax wrap or a clean shower cap and place somewhere warm for 2 hours.

6. Once about doubled in size, knock the air out of the dough. To knock the air back you can take it out of the bowl, or keep it in the bowl and give it a few gentle punches, then knead gently for up to 2 minutes. Use your electric mixer and dough hook if this part is not great for your hands or arms. Divide into 12 by eye or I find they weigh roughly 88g each.

7. Like my other recipes I like to shape each bun by pulling the dough outwards into a flattish circle shape. I then go clockwise, folding the outer edge bit by bit into the centre of the circle. Then turn it over and roll the base gently so you have a tidy seam underneath and place onto the baking sheet or tray. Leave them about 2cm apart or more.

8. Cover the buns with a clean **damp** tea towel or place inside a clean proving bag, trap the air in and clip the end to keep it tight. Rest for another hour, depending on the time of year and heat of your kitchen. About 15 minutes before baking, preheat the oven to 180°C fan/200°C/gas 6. When these have grown nicely to at least double in size you can glaze them with the beaten egg or a little sunflower oil and sprinkle with the onion seeds.

9. Place in the oven and bake for 15-20 minutes, turning the baking sheets trays round halfway through for even colouring, or swap the two trays' shelves. The final burger buns should be a deep brown and sound hollow when tapped on the base.

10. Once out of the oven, place the buns on cooling racks.

We like to slice these and griddle them before filling with our burger or barbecue creations. Spiced gherkins and melted cheese are a must.

One Hundred Per Cent Wholemeal

Beginner

I really enjoy wholemeal and I find it fuels my energy levels for longer than white bread. One thing you need to know when buying wholemeal bread in Britain is that unless all the flour used is 100% wholemeal flour, it should not be labelled as wholemeal bread. It's worth checking the ingredients on labels and the Government legislation for further explanation. But better yet, you can make your own and know exactly what's in it! This is a straightforward recipe I enjoy making as delicious sliced loaves for home. I love it with butter and marmalade.

This makes 2 loaves of 2lb tin size

Ingredients

- 1kg strong wholemeal bread flour

- 4g sugar

- 6g fast action yeast

- 700g tepid water – 150g of just boiled water and 550g cold water

- 12g salt

- 28g sunflower or other vegetable oil

- Sunflower or other vegetable oil of your choice to grease the tins

Extra Utensils

- Optional - Electric hand mixer or free-standing mixer with dough hook/s and large bowl

- 2 x 2lb loaf tins

- Optional - Water sprayer with fresh cold tap water inside

Method

1. Add to your mixing bowl the flour, sugar and yeast and give them a stir with a wooden spoon to mix evenly.

2. Add the weighed tepid water to the dry mixture and as you start to stir add the salt in too.

3. You should have a lumpy mixture that you can now add the oil to. Continue to mix until it comes together as a smoother dough. Use a mixer with a dough hook if you find this easier and mix for about 1 minute.

4. Next place the dough in a lightly oiled large bowl. Place a clean shower cap, a wax wrap or oiled cling film over the bowl, tightly. Place this somewhere warm for an hour or until it has doubled. Take a photo if this helps to compare the size doubling.

5. When the dough has almost doubled, grease the 2 loaf tins with the oil.

6. Place the dough on a very lightly floured surface and knead for about 1 minute.

7. Next we will shape the 2 loaves and put them in the tins to prove again. Divide the dough with a large knife or dough cutter into roughly 2 even pieces. Shape each dough piece gently into a ball. Then make it into a long shape by pulling each side outwards. Then fold each end into the middle and gently roll it into a sausage type shape, with a seam underneath.

8. Put each dough into a loaf tin with the seam underneath. Place a clean tea towel over the tins and put them somewhere warm to rise for roughly 45 minutes to an hour.

9. Near the end of proving time preheat the oven for at least 15 minutes to 200°C fan/220°C/gas 7.

10. Take off the tea towel and bake the loaves for roughly 40 minutes until a golden colour and the bottom sounds hollow when tapped. This bit I never could get to grips with, so carefully (using oven gloves) hold the top of the loaf while you tip it upside down and hold it in the oven glove. Knock on the bottom of the loaf with your knuckle and if it feels hard, rather than soggy, and makes a 'knocking' noise then it's cooked. If it doesn't make a knocking noise, return it to the tin and bake for 5-10 more minutes and test again.

11. Put the loaves on a wire rack to cool, out of their tins. You can spray the loaf with a few squirts of clean water and this brings a sheen to the top crust of the loaf.

Enjoy sliced for your everyday sandwiches or as toast with your favourite spreads and toppings.

Keep airtight for 3 days or it freezes well for up to a month.

The Buttie Satisfier – White Tin Loaf

Beginner

It's the weekend. We need a white buttie loaf. I do enjoy making
this for my family and I enjoy a slice or two with a fried egg and
tomato sauce sandwiched between. It's a proper white loaf. Not an
undercooked, doughy, mass-produced tummy ache creator (in my
opinion). Feel smug when serving this up as the real deal. It has a lovely
yellowy colour when made with organic white bread flour. You can
try it out with different white bread flours from local producers.
It's suitable for dairy and egg free diets.

This makes 2 loaves of 2lb tin size

Ingredients

- 1kg strong white bread flour

- 6g fast action yeast

- 8g caster sugar

- 645g tepid water – 145g of just
  boiled water and 500g cold water

- 30g sunflower or other vegetable oil

- 16g salt

- Extra sunflower or other vegetable
  oil of your choice to grease the tins

Extra Utensils

- Optional - Electric hand mixer or
  free-standing mixer with dough
  hook/s and large bowl

- 2 x 2lb loaf tins

- Optional - Water sprayer with
  fresh cold tap water inside

Method

1. In a large mixing bowl, add the flour, yeast and sugar. Mix evenly together with a wooden spoon or electric mixer.

2. Add the water and oil to the dry mixture and as you do so, add the salt too.

3. Mix by hand with a wooden spoon or use an electric mixer with a dough hook until it comes together as a lumpy mixture.

4. Next, use the kneading tips on pages 9 and 10, if you'd like some guidance here. It doesn't need a lot of kneading. So, 3 minutes by hand should be fine or 2 minutes with the dough hook and electric mixer on a medium speed.

5. Put the dough in a lightly oiled bowl and cover with a wax wrap, clean tea towel or cling film and put it in a warm place for 60-90 minutes. A warm place can be found in an airing cupboard, proving drawer or in the oven with just the oven light on. No direct heat.

6. When your dough has roughly doubled in size it should feel and look puffier. We can knock the air out of the dough ready for putting in the tin and the second prove. To knock the air out you can take it out of the bowl, or keep it in the bowl and give it a few gentle punches, then knead gently for up to 2 minutes. Use your electric mixer and dough hook if this part is not great for your hands or arms.

7. Now it's time to divide the dough in half, using the edge of a dough scraper or a high-sided knife. Then grease each tin well with the oil of your choice.

8. Now it's shaping time before placing in the tins. This is always a good opportunity to develop your shaping skills. It doesn't have to be perfect each time as you will still get a lovely tin loaf.

9. Get one of the two doughs. I like to pull it into a flattish rectangle and then fold the 2 ends into the centre. Then roll the dough part nearest you over onto the opposite edge and tuck it under as you go. So, the seam is at the base and you have an even unbroken surface to the dough.

10. Gently lift it and place it seam side down into one of the tins. It then has room to grow at the next prove. Repeat with the other dough piece and tin.

11. Place a clean tea towel over both tins and allow to rise somewhere warm for

an hour. By this time the top will have risen above the top of the loaf tin. It will rise a little more when baking too.

12. About 15 minutes before the end of this second prove, preheat your oven to 200°C fan/220°C/gas 7.

13. To bake, place the 2 tins on the middle oven shelf with a gap in between them and bake for about 40 minutes. Check the loaves after 30 minutes to see if you need to turn them round to bake evenly. If they're getting too brown, turn the oven down to 180°C fan /200°C/gas 6 for the last 10 minutes.

14. When baked they should sound hollow when tapped. (see my tip for step 11 on page 69).

15. Once baked put the loaves on a cooling rack out of their tins and allow to cool fully. For a slight sheen on top, you can spray a mist of water over each loaf as soon as they come out of the oven. They'll look very fancy!

Enjoy for butties, doorstep sandwiches, toast, toasties and more.

Loaf of Deep Rye

Beginner

Something that educated me about what customers enjoyed at some market sales, was the desire for rye loaves. And many people who asked me for rye sourdough or rye tin loaves wanted as much rye flour as possible in there. It goes really well with eggs, smoked salmon, vegan scrambled egg and soft cheeses. This loaf I make here has gathered feedback such as, 'nice and moist, with a wonderful flavour of a summer hay meadow'. That comment is so inviting. So, if you like rye or enjoy the deep, dark loaves, give this recipe a try. It's fairly straightforward and I'm sure it could be adapted to use with other dark flours.

This makes 2 loaves of 2lb tin size

Ingredients

- 800g dark rye flour

- 400g white strong bread flour

- 9g fast action yeast

- 8g unrefined sugar or caster sugar

- 60g black treacle

- 200g recently boiled water

- 600g cold tap water

- 12g salt

- 56g sunflower oil or other vegetable oil

- Additional flour for dusting surfaces

- Sunflower or other vegetable oil of your choice to grease the tins

Extra Utensils

- Optional - Electric hand mixer or free-standing mixer with dough hook/s and large bowl

- Optional - gloves for sticky dough

- 2 x 2lb loaf tins

Method

1. Into your mixing bowl or electric mixer bowl place both flours and add the yeast and sugar and give them a stir with a wooden spoon to mix evenly.

2. In a measuring jug mix the treacle with the freshly boiled water until it's dissolved. Then add all the cold water to it.

3. Add the wet mixture to the dry mixture and as you start to stir or mix with a dough hook, add the salt in too.

4. You should have a lumpy mixture that you can now add the oil to. Continue to mix until it comes together as a smoother dough. Use the mixer with a dough hook or do this by hand for about 1 minute.

5. Next place the dough in a lightly oiled large bowl to double in size. Place a clean shower cap, a wax wrap or oiled cling film over the bowl tightly. Place this somewhere warm for an hour or until it has doubled. Take a photo if this helps to compare the size doubling.

6. When the dough has almost doubled, grease the 2 tins with the oil.

7. Place the dough on a very lightly floured surface and knead for about 1 minute or do this with the electric mixer and dough hook.

8. To shape the dough, cut it evenly in half. It will be sticky from the treacle, so you can use food safe gloves here or just allow your hands to get a bit coated.

9. Lightly flour the surface again, if needed. Then fold the outsides of the dough into the middle until you have done this all the way round in a clockwise manner. It will look fairly round. Then roll it over a couple of times to get a tin-sized sausage shape.

10. Put each dough into a loaf tin with the seam underneath. Place a clean tea towel over the tins and put them somewhere warm to rise for roughly 45 minutes to an hour.

11. Near the end of proving time preheat the oven for at least 15 minutes to 200°C fan/220°C/gas 7.

12. Take off the tea towel and bake the loaves for roughly 40-45 minutes until it is a golden colour and the bottom sounds hollow when tapped. (See my tip from step 10 on page 69.)

13. Put the loaves on a wire rack to cool, out of their tins. You can spray each loaf with a few squirts of clean water and this brings a crust to the loaf. Or you can brush with a little sunflower oil for a light shine.

Enjoy sliced thinly with contrasting flavours and textures. Cream cheese is very effective. Perhaps smoked mackerel or hummus would work well too.

Keep airtight for 3 days or it freezes well for up to a month.

Spelt Bread Rolls

Beginner

I like making these because the brown spelt flour makes a really delicious roll, but I also find this a fairly easy recipe with quite instant results. Spelt flour is a wholewheat flour made from the entire grain. It is said that the gluten in spelt is more water soluble than modern types of wheat. I don't make any scientific claims, but you can do some research online and make up your own mind. Some people enjoy it because it has a fuller flavour, which is probably due to using the entire grain. The addition of honey in this recipe brings a subtle sweetness that is just right for a dinner roll or to dunk in soup. You can use agave syrup if you want a vegan roll. For gluten free, you can try a brown gluten free flour, a gluten free yeast and oats.

This makes 10 rolls

Ingredients

- 600g brown spelt flour (you can use white spelt flour. It may need less water)

- 7g fast action yeast

- 300g tepid water

- 45g olive oil (not extra virgin) plus extra for brushing

- 2 tsp table salt

- 2 tbsp honey or agave syrup

- Rolled oats to top (optional)

Extra Utensils

- Optional - Electric mixer and dough hook

Method

1. Mix the spelt flour with the yeast in a mixing bowl with a wooden spoon or in an electric mixer with dough hook.

2. Add the water, followed by the olive oil, table salt and honey. Mix very well with a wooden spoon until it's a smooth dough. Or in the electric mixer for about 5 minutes.

3. Lightly flour your work surface and then knead for about 2 minutes. If this is something you find hard to do, you can mix for another 2 minutes in the stand mixer or with the handheld mixer.

4. Then, put the dough in the mixing bowl, cover with a tea towel and leave to rest for about an hour. We are looking for it to double in size. If it's a cold day you can place the bowl somewhere warm.

5. Once risen to double the size, divide the dough into 10, or do mini versions of 20. Roll into spheres and keep the seam underneath. Place on a lined baking sheet, about 1 cm apart. Sprinkle a few rolled oats onto the top of each one (optional). Cover with a clean tea towel. Leave to rise for an hour, somewhere warm again or on the counter top if it's a warm day.

6. About half an hour before baking, preheat the oven to 200°C fan/220°C/ gas 7. Place the rolls in the oven and bake for 15-20 minutes. They should look golden brown and puffed up.

7. Remove from the oven and gently brush on olive oil or a melted butter of your choice. Allow to cool on a wire rack and then serve. These last in an airtight container for about 3 days. They can be frozen for up to a month.

Garlic & Herb Milk Bread Twists

Intermediate

Here I'm proud to bring you a recipe created from my grandmother's
1930s recipe book. Within it she documented recipes, learned in
her employment making large catering amounts of classic dishes,
preserves, pickles, cakes, bread and so much more. I've incorporated
some of my own soft dough knowledge to bring a soft bread twist
that goes really well with any pasta dish or as a starter with a dip.
My homemade pizza sauce goes very well (page 45). There are options
here to make the dough recipe vegan too. This will become a family
favourite, I guarantee. If possible, use a mixer, as the dough is quite wet
until the twisting stage, but the reward is a softer dough as a result.

This makes 10 large twists

Ingredients

- 475g warm milk – semi-skimmed,
  whole, soya or oat work well. Warm
  in a microwave for 30 seconds or in a
  pan on a hob very gently, until it is just
  beginning to warm. Hot or boiling milk
  will not activate the yeast

- 5g fast action yeast

- 615g strong white bread flour, plus
  extra plain flour for dusting

- 1 large or medium egg or egg substitute

- 1 tsp table salt

- 25g unsalted butter or plant butter
  (not spread) – room temperature cut
  into small cubes

- 3 tsp dried oregano

- 2 tsp garlic granules

- 1 tsp dried or freshly chopped parsley

- 1 tsp flaked salt

- 45g unsalted butter or plant butter
  for brushing - melted

Extra Utensils

- Whisk or fork

- Ideal but optional - Electric hand mixer
  or free standing mixer with dough
  hook/s and large bowl

- 2 small bowls

- Pastry brush

Method

1. Into your mixing bowl place the warmed milk – see the instructions in the ingredients list. Add the yeast and mix with a whisk or fork and leave to stand for 5 minutes.

2. Next add the flour, egg or egg substitute and salt and mix until it comes together. Then mix on a medium speed with a dough hook for about 3 minutes, or mix in a bowl with a spoon or by hand for 5 minutes until you get a smooth but wettish dough.

3. Next add the cubes of butter one by one and mix in until combined. This part will be very messy and gloopy but it will come together. If doing this by hand then use a wooden spoon and a mixing bowl to keep the mess together. Once the butter is mixed in well keep mixing for about 5 minutes, using the stand mixer with the dough hook. Or 8 minutes by hand in the mixing bowl or on a surface.

4. After this time place the dough into a lightly oiled mixing bowl and cover with something airtight like a clean shower cap, wax wrap or recyclable cling film. Place somewhere warm for an hour – for tips see the ciabatta recipe on page 95.

5. Once about doubled in size preheat the oven for at least 15 minutes while you do the next step to 200°C fan/220°C/gas 7. Then scrape the dough out gently onto a well-floured worktop. While keeping it as puffy as possible, use your hands to fashion it into a rectangle. No need to stretch or flatten it. Sprinkle the oregano evenly onto the surface of the dough.

6. Look at the dough and work out where to divide to get roughly 10 twists. I plan 5 long lines of dough that can be cut in half to make 10. Then do a little score with a knife or dough divider to mark it.

7. Cut one of the pieces near to you and then hold at each end. Twist each end in opposite directions until it's about 20cm long and got a good twist all the way along. As you do so, the oregano will twist in too.

8. Place 5 per baking tray with space between, or if they fit, place all 10 on a baking sheet. Both lined with a silicone sheet or greased and lined with greaseproof paper.

9. Place in the oven and turn it down to 180°C fan/200°C/gas 6. Bake for 15–20 minutes, turning the baking sheet trays round halfway through for even colouring. Or swap the oven shelves for the 2 trays.

10. While the twists are in the oven, mix together the garlic granules, parsley and salt in a small bowl. About 5 minutes before removing the twists from the oven, gently melt the second quantity of butter. Do this by placing the butter in a small bowl and microwave on 30-second blasts or in a small pan on the hob. Remove from the heat.

11. Once out of the oven, place the baking sheet or trays with the twists on cooling racks. Then brush each twist generously with the melted butter, followed by a generous sprinkle of the herb and garlic mix.

These are fantastic served warm, 5 or 10 minutes after removing from the oven. Or you can reheat them on a baking sheet or tray for 10 minutes at 180°C fan/200°C/gas 6, in a preheated oven. The microwave for 10-15 seconds, for 1 or 2 twists, will heat them gently too. They will keep in an airtight container for up to 3 days. Wrap tightly and freeze for up to 1 month.

Stuffed Loaf

This recipe is great for a picnic or a weekend lunch. I planned this
recipe to make whilst volunteering at a local alternative provision and
day centre. Actually, it may have been part of my first explorations into
bread, thinking about it now. The cooking tutor was on leave and
I was asked to explore what students would like to make. Bread was
the answer and what fun we had making this, slapping the doughy
mass on the metal counter, until it became smooth and stretchy.
A lot of energy was generated that day and the resulting concertina
of stuffed bread was delicious. The appearance of one did look like
the derrière of a large animal. And so we called it 'bottoms up bread'!

This makes enough for 2 loaves

Ingredients

- 60g unsalted butter or plant butter - melted

- 200g whole milk or plant milk at room temperature

- 7g fast action yeast

- 1 tbsp granulated sugar

- 1 large egg – lightly beaten or egg substitute

- 500g strong white bread flour. Keep 100g more nearby, in case needed during mixing

- 1 tbsp table salt

Topping

- 1 egg yolk mixed with 1 tsp tap water, or use sunflower oil

- 1 tsp onion seeds (optional)

Filling ideas

- 200g sliced or grated extra mature Cheddar, halloumi, feta or plant cheese of your choice.

- Olives, sundried tomatoes, roasted peppers.

- Fresh or dried herbs.

Extra Utensils

- Small bowl

- Optional - Electric mixer with a dough hook

- Heavy baking sheet or roasting tin (larger than 20cm x 25cm)

Method

1. First melt the butter until it is only just melted, either in a pan on the hob or in the microwave. Make sure it's not hot. Put to one side.

2. In a large mixing bowl, place the room temperature milk. Add the yeast and sugar. Stir with a fork or little whisk to disperse the yeast.

3. Add the beaten egg to this mixture, followed by the melted butter. Mix gently with your wooden spoon and put to one side for 5 minutes, until it is foamy.

4. Add 500g of bread flour to your large mixing bowl. Pour in the yeast mixture steadily. Combine the mixture using your wooden spoon or electric mixer and add the salt as you mix.

5. Scrape any flour from the side of the bowl back into the mixture. Continue to mix for 2 minutes. If needed, add 1 to 3 tbsp of flour, a little at a time. You will end up with a smooth dough. Less is more!

6. Bring the dough together into a ball with your hands. It's time to start kneading now. Use the tips section of this book for kneading ideas on pages 9 and 10 or just go with 'stretch and fold' or 'whack and fold', depending on today's mood! The dough will be soft, elastic and a bit sticky. If it is too sticky it may need a little more flour added in, but just add a little at a time.

7. Place the dough in a lightly oiled bowl. Cover with a damp clean tea towel or cling film. Leave it in a warm place for about an hour or until doubled in size. Depending on the weather, this could take up to 2 hours.

8. Have a little wash up and tidy away. And definitely have a pat on the back for your work so far and a drink of your choice. Mine's tea! Slice any cheese and get any other filling ingredients ready during this time. Or use this time for getting on with your day.

9. After the dough has doubled in size punch down the bread and knead it in the bowl for a few seconds. No need to over knead here. You've done the hard mixing already!

10. Flour the work surface and place the dough on it. Cut the dough into 2. With the rolling pin, roll one of the doughs into a rectangle shape. Not too thin. I would say approximately 30cm x 15cm.

11. Add your chosen filling and leave a 2cm gap around each straight edge. With your hands, roll the dough from the longer edge towards the opposite long edge, so you have what looks like a large sausage roll. Keep the seam underneath and tuck the 2 open ends underneath.

12. Push the long sausage into shape, like a concertina 'z' or 's' shape. Push together gently. Lift your loaf, that now looks more rounded, carefully onto a greased and lined baking sheet. Keep the loaf together snugly.

13. Repeat with your second loaf onto another baking sheet or tray – you can change your filling here if you like. This is also a great chance to refine what you have just learned. Or if the roll didn't go as planned, to have another go!

14. Cover both loaves loosely with clean tea towels. And allow to sit at room temperature or somewhere warm for 30 minutes.

15. After 15 minutes, preheat the oven to 190°C fan/210°C/gas 7.

Bake

1. Brush the loaves with egg wash or oil and sprinkle with onion seeds if required.

2. Bake in the preheated oven for 30 to 35 mins. If baking 2, you may need to add a further 5-10 minutes. Smell that bread! Turn your oven down to 170°C fan/190°C/gas 5 for the last 10 minutes if it is too brown, but it will go fairly dark on top, so this is up to you.

3. Once golden brown and baked, remove the breads from the oven and leave on the sheet or trays. Gently check the underside of the bread – if it is pale then it may not be cooked through, so give it 5 or 10 more minutes in the oven. Because of the filling we just want to make sure it is cooked.

4. Place the sheet or trays on cooling racks. Allow to cool for at least 10 minutes before you attempt to cut one. It's hard to wait this long with that wonderful smell, I know!

Enjoy warm or allow to cool fully. Once fully cooled it can be kept wrapped in the fridge for 2 to 3 days. Or perhaps you'd like to give one as a gift.

Maneesh Style Flatbreads

Intermediate

'Could you make 18 Maneesh style flatbreads for a dining booking next week?' I was once asked this by a private chef. Well, I wasn't sure I could do it. It's amazing, though, how some of our great achievements happen when the pressure is on. My love for new creations and my eagerness to delight led me to create this recipe. My research involved trying a few recipes and adapting them to be free of sesame and just the right texture and size. They had to be quite big, so I started off by trialling 2 at a time. These worked well. Not surprisingly, 18 generous flatbreads took me most of the day and evening to make, roll out, top and bake. Don't worry, it certainly won't take you more than 2 hours to make 2 to 4 of these.

I thoroughly enjoyed the experience and my family and I enjoyed topping the baked Maneesh style bread with hummus, feta, pomegranate, roasted butternut, rocket and mint. For a meaty version you can try making a Middle Eastern style minced lamb topping with mint, nutmeg and cinnamon.

This makes 2 large (tortilla sized) flatbreads. Double the recipe for 4.

Ingredients

- 400g strong white bread flour
- 7g fast action yeast
- 250g warm, but not hot, water – add 100g just boiled water to 150g cold tap water
- 13g olive oil (not extra virgin)
- 6g salt

Extra Utensils

- 1 small bowl
- Optional – Electric mixer with dough hook and large bowl
- Rolling pin

Topping – Za'atar style, without sesame

- 1 tsp dried oregano
- 1 tsp dried marjoram
- 1 tsp sumac
- 1 tsp dried thyme
- 6g table salt
- 18g olive oil – regular is ideal

Method

1. Place the flour and yeast in the mixing bowl and use a wooden spoon to mix evenly.

2. Next add the water, oil and salt and mix the dough until it is fairly smooth. You can do this by hand or in a stand mixer or with an electric mixer with a dough hook.

3. Next, lightly flour the work surface and knead the dough by hand for about 4 minutes. A dough scraper will help to push it from the work surface, if it sticks. Or use the mixer with the dough hook for 3 minutes. The dough should start to become stretchy, but will still be quite wet.

4. Place the dough in a lightly oiled bowl. Cover with a clean shower cap, wax wrap or lightly oiled cling film and put it somewhere warm for about an hour.

5. While the dough is proving use this time to mix together the herbs, salt and oil for the topping. Leave to one side in a bowl.

6. Once the dough has roughly doubled in size put the bowl of dough on the worktop and knock the air out by pushing into it a few times.

7. Then place the dough on a lightly floured work surface or back in the electric mixer bowl and knead by hand or with the dough hook on the mixer for about 3 minutes.

8. Cut the dough into 2 even pieces and make each into a ball shape.

9. Put each flatbread on a greased and lined baking sheet or tray. Using a rolling pin, roll each dough to a round shape that is roughly the size of a large flat tortilla wrap (dinner plate size). Use flour if it sticks to the rolling pin. Allow the flatbreads to rest for 30 minutes covered with a tea towel and preheat your oven to 210°C fan /230°C/gas 8.

10. When you're ready, top each flatbread with the za'atar style topping and bake for about 15 minutes. They will look a wonderful deep golden colour. Remove from the oven and place on a wire rack to cool.

11. Top with your chosen goodies, as I've suggested at the top of this recipe or use them as an enjoyable tear and dip bread.

These are at their very best on the day. You can store them airtight for the following day. They can be frozen if wrapped well and used within 1 month. Once defrosted, I'd recommend warming them gently in the oven with a sprinkling of cold tap water on top for about 8 minutes on 180°C fan/200°C/gas 6.

Ciabatta Sticks or Rolls

Intermediate

My best advice for ciabatta is handle it as little as possible. This is a
very, very wet dough. If you approach it with this in mind, then you
will learn not to be thrown by it. The moisture content is necessary
for the best results. By the afternoon you'll be dipping it in balsamic
and oil or slicing horizontally for a really delicious Mediterranean
style type sandwich. Or make your own soup and dip it in for a 100%
homemade meal. Go on, show it who's boss and give it a go.

This makes 3 medium sticks or 6 rolls

Ingredients

- 500g strong white bread flour

- 10g fast action yeast

- 400g room temperature water - mostly
  cold with a dash of recently boiled

- 37g olive oil (not extra virgin)

- 10g table salt

- Plain white flour for lots of dusting
  before baking

Extra Utensils

- Medium / large rectangular
  plastic tub

- Ideal but optional - Electric mixer
  with dough hook and large bowl

Method

1. Weigh all your ingredients ready for use.

2. Rub a small layer of oil over the inside of the plastic tub, using additional olive oil.

3. In the mixing bowl add the flour and the yeast and mix together thoroughly with a spoon. This avoids clumps of yeast.

4. Add approximately 300g of the water, then the 37g olive oil and the salt.

5. Mix slowly with your chosen mixer and add the remaining 100g of water as you do it.

6. Keep mixing on a midway speed for at least 5 minutes. The dough will still be very wet when you've finished, just a little stringier.

7. Place all of this dough into the oiled tub and scrape the sides of the mixing bowl out, to use as much dough as you can. The dough will at least double in size, so make sure it has room to grow.

8. On a hot day you can drape your clean tea towel over the top and leave it on the worktop for about 2 hours. In colder temperatures place it in the oven with only the oven light on and the tea towel over the tub (not any additional oven heating). If this isn't enough to grow it, you can carefully place an oven roasting tin of freshly boiled water well below it in the oven to help raise the temperature. Again, I state here that no oven heat should be on.

9. If you have a warm airing cupboard or even a proving drawer, place in there and check after 2 hours or maybe less.

10. Once doubled in size, prepare your baking sheet or tray and oven. Preheat the oven to 200°C fan/220°C/gas 7. Get a large baking sheet or 2 trays and line with a little oil, greaseproof paper or a reusable silicone liner.

11. Now, get ready here. The tipping out part is where we want to handle this dough the least, or it just ends up sticking to your hands and losing its lovely gas bubbles. Don't worry.

12. Put a good layer of the plain white flour on your clean work surface. About the same shape as the base of the plastic tub you're using.

13. Put your baking trays or sheet directly next to the flour and have your knife or dough divider at the ready.

14. Tip the dough very gently onto your floured worktop and let it come out itself. Any parts left on the sides can be encouraged out quickly, but watch out as it is very sticky.

15. Let the rectangle of dough settle for a few seconds in front of you. Sprinkle with a generous amount of plain flour. It will be almost impossible to handle. Look at its shape and work out where you will divide it. Either to make 3 or to make 6. So, score it with 2 even lines horizontally, to make 3 pieces. To make 6, lightly score 1 line along the middle after scoring the first 2 lines as explained.

16. Next you are going to sharply cut the dough on your scoring lines with the cutting utensil.

For the ciabatta sticks, scoop up 1 piece with the flat of your wide utensil and use both hands. With either side supporting it swiftly, as you lift it near to the baking tray, pull each end out slightly to a longer shape, just before you place it on the tray. You have 1 stick. You can pat it a little each side to help straighten it, but not too much. The more you make these, the more this part becomes second nature. Repeat with the 2 other pieces of dough, leaving 6cm between each one on the sheet or use 2 baking trays.

For the ciabatta rolls, do the same scooping technique, but there is no need to stretch the dough as you place it on the sheet or trays. Position the dough rolls with enough space between them not to leak into each other. Each should be a rough, small rectangular shape.

17. Sprinkle the doughs with a good amount of the plain flour if needed and cover with a clean tea towel and leave to sit for 15 minutes.

18. When you are ready to bake, place the sheet or trays in the oven and bake for between 15 and 25 minutes. I say this because it depends on the width you have shaped each stick or roll into. We're looking for a golden brown colour and cooked through to the centre.

19. Once baked, place on a rack to cool.

These are at their very best on the day, but can be wrapped tightly and kept for 3 days or frozen for up to 1 month. Warm a little after defrosting.

Keep making them and the handling part becomes easier each time, as you get to know what to expect.

Sticky Cinnamon Buns

Intermediate

When you get that urge for a soft doughy treat, I've found that these sticky cinnamon buns hit the right spot. I like to make them quite large, so you get a good portion, but you can cut them smaller if you want more, which is always pleasing to have. So, isn't it easier to just buy one at a supermarket? Well, the answer is yes, that may be easier. But you can have fun making these fresh sticky buns of loveliness and you can adapt them to how you enjoy them. I have given the option for filling with sultanas, if you prefer that. And I have also added a tablespoon of fed white sourdough starter when adding the milk into the mixture. It makes them slightly stickier to roll out but it does make the taste and pull apart texture divine.

This makes 12-16 buns

Ingredients

- 810g French type 55 flour or strong white bread flour

- 7g fast action yeast

- 80g caster sugar

- 255g room temperature whole milk or plant milk – I have used oat and soya

- 255g tepid water

- 1 tbsp fed white sourdough starter (optional)

- 15g table salt

- 80g unsalted butter or plant butter (not spread) – room temperature cut into small cubes

Icing Drizzle

- 200g icing sugar

- 2 tbsp just boiled water. Add 1 tsp or more water gradually to make a more watery glaze

- Beaten egg or sunflower oil (1 tbsp) (optional)

Filling

- 2 tsp ground cinnamon

- 70g light brown soft sugar

- 60g room temperature butter

OR for a Chelsea style bun:

- 150g-200g sultanas instead of the above filling

Extra Utensils

- Whisk or fork

- Ideal but optional - Electric hand mixer or free-standing mixer with dough hook/s, balloon whisks and large bowl

- Large ruler or tape measure

- Rolling pin

- Pastry brush

Method

1. Into your mixing bowl place the flour, yeast and sugar and mix gently until well dispersed.

2. Next add the milk, water (and sourdough starter option) and salt and mix with a wooden spoon or on a medium speed with a dough hook for about 2–3 minutes. It should come together as a smooth dough. Continue to mix on a medium speed in the mixer for 2 more minutes. If doing by hand, then you can remove it from the bowl and slap and fold it on the worktop. It may get sticky, so just use a dough scraper or a similar fine edged tool like a hard spatula to scrape it off the worktop. It can be great fun and very therapeutic.

3. Next add the cubes of butter one by one and mix in until incorporated. Again, this will get very messy and gloopy but it will come together. If doing this by hand then continue on the worktop until well mixed or use a wooden spoon and a mixing bowl to keep the mess together. Sometimes the play and mess aspect are exactly what we're looking for, so dive in. Once the butter is mixed in well keep mixing for about 5 minutes, in the stand mixer with the dough hook. Or knead by hand in the mixing bowl or on a surface for as long as you can. Slap and fold. Or stretch and fold. The oiliness should reduce to give you a smooth dough again.

4. Many bakers like to test the stretch of the dough using the 'window pane' test at this point. I have done this, then at other times I've been in a rush to get it done. Either way I haven't noticed a huge difference in the end result. But if you want to do it, just grab a small section of dough and stretch it out. If you can see through the dough slightly that's the window pane. If it breaks and tears immediately then it isn't a window pane. Knead it a bit more but don't pressure yourself to do too much. Save those poor arms!

5. Next, place the dough into a lightly oiled mixing bowl and cover with something airtight like a clean shower cap, wax wrap or recyclable cling film. Place somewhere warm for an hour – for tips see my ciabatta recipe on page 95.

6. While the dough is rising, mix your cinnamon filling ingredients together with an electric mixer and balloon whisks or by hand with the back of a wooden spoon, flattening it and then stirring to fluff it up just a little. Or weigh out your sultanas for the Chelsea style bun.

7. Once doubled in size it's time to roll out, fill and cut the sweet buns of loveliness. Scrape the dough out gently onto a floured worktop. I don't punch out the air, because this happens as we roll it. Punching out the air makes it harder to roll – I've been there and it is just frustrating.

8. So, we're going to roll the dough into a rectangle shape, roughly 50cm x 35cm, with the longer edge nearest your

tummy and the shorter edges going up each side. You can use a ruler or tape measure here or guestimate it if you're good with measurements. Roll the dough a little bit forwards, then a little bit toward each side and repeat until you get the rough size with an even depth. If it's sticking to the worktop, gently lift a corner and powder some flour under the sticky bits. Ends can be trimmed to make a rectangle but try not to cut much off as this takes away from your precious buns.

9. Use your cinnamon filling mixture now and carefully spread it out using a bendy thin spatula if you have one. And leave about 1cm gap round all 4 edges. Or sprinkle the sultanas evenly over the dough.

10. To roll up, start from the longer edge nearest your tummy. Ease it up all the way along gradually until you get the first roll. Then check it is fairly even and continue to roll over, snugly. Not super tight and not too loose, until it reaches the other long edge furthest away from you. Carefully tuck the seam underneath all the way along.

11. The last step before the second prove is nearly here and then you can have a well-deserved rest. Get your ruler / tape measure and dough cutter or wide bladed large knife ready. Measure 3.5cm and do a gentle score line. If you want smaller buns, measure in 2.5cm gaps. Repeat until you have between 12 and 16 bun measurements. Then have your greased and lined baking trays or baking sheet at the ready. Cut straight down each scoring line in a fairly quick movement, taking care with the cutting blade. Place each bun swirl side upwards on the baking sheet or tray with about 1cm space between each. You can do this on 1 or 2 trays. It will be a bit like a grid of cinnamon buns in straight lines. You'll get an even rise and bake then.

12. Cover the buns with a clean damp tea towel or place inside a clean proving bag, trap the air in and clip the end to keep it tight. Rest for 90 minutes to 3 hours, depending on the time of year and heat of your kitchen. About 15 minutes before baking, preheat the oven to 180°C fan/200°C/gas 6. When these have grown nicely to at least double you can bake. If you do not wish to ice them but would like a nice glaze, use the beaten egg or sunflower oil to brush over the top of the dough before baking. Leave this step out if you're icing them.

13. Place in the oven and bake for 15–20 minutes and turn the baking sheet trays round halfway through for even colouring, or swap oven shelves for the 2 trays.

14. Once out of the oven, place the baking sheet or trays on cooling racks. When fully cooled, top with icing by mixing to a slightly runny consistency and no lumps. Or leave as they are.

Enjoy wholeheartedly.

Teacakes for Toasting

Beginner to Intermediate

When I worked in a quaint café in the market town of Bewdley, I had my first job in a professional kitchen. When staff were short, you'd find me attempting the barista and service roles too. In the kitchen, we would start early on softening the onions for the daily quiche, making and rolling buttery pastry, cutting fresh puffy rounds of scones, whilst prepping fresh sandwich fillings, washing and chopping crunchy salad and cooking up creative soups. If there was time, we'd make sponges ready for cooling, then speedily fill and top them in the afternoon, which was always a highlight of the day. An instant, gorgeous edible creation. And I was motivated by the owner's enthusiasm for all things cake and sweet stuff. And she won't mind me saying that she was equally motivated to try creations we'd come up with. That's one of the reasons we became good friends. But the teacakes! They were an issue to toast. Dare to take your eye off the ball and they would burn. I enjoy making these from scratch as they aren't too difficult. I recommend toasting these under the grill and refraining from multi-tasking until the teacake has made its official entrance to the plate!

This makes 8 teacakes. Double it up for 16 and freeze some.

Ingredients

- 500g strong white bread flour

- 10g fast action yeast

- 1 tsp mixed spice

- 55g caster sugar

- 55g unsalted butter or plant butter (not spread) – room temperature cut into small cubes

- 300g tepid water

- 8g salt

- 120g sultanas

- 1 medium egg beaten or plant oil like sunflower for brushing

Extra Utensils

- Optional - electric hand mixer or free-standing mixer with dough hook/s and large bowl

- Pastry brush

Method

1. Into your mixing bowl place the flour, yeast, spice and sugar and mix gently until well dispersed.

2. Next add the butter, water and salt and mix with a wooden spoon or on a medium speed with a dough hook for about 2 minutes. It should come together as a rough dough. I don't usually suggest adding more bread flour, but if it is very wet add a small amount like 10-20g.

3. You have the choice of kneading by hand or with the electric mixer on medium with the dough hook for 5 minutes. To knead by hand just stretch the dough on the floured surface, fold and slap it on the worktop. I know, it is so fun and silly! If it's very sticky, just use your dough scraper to keep scraping it off the worktop and bringing it back together and it will get smoother and smoother. If you don't have a dough scraper use a fine plastic or silicone spatula.

4. Okay, enough of this part, let's give it a rest in a lightly oiled bowl and you know this bit by now: cover with something airtight like a clean shower cap, wax wrap or recyclable cling film. Place somewhere warm for 2 hours. Maybe less on a hot day.

5. Once about doubled in size add the sultanas and knead evenly into the dough. This is fun dispersing these around the puffy dough.

6. Next get your baking sheet or trays that are greased and lined. I like to get an even size on the teacakes, so I weigh the dough and divide the amount by 8. Or you can simply separate the dough into 8 by eye. It's up to you.

7. Lightly flour the worktop and have your scales to hand on zero. Cut a blob off and make the amount up to your desired bun amount. Do this 8 times.

8. To shape the buns, pull the dough outwards into a flattish circle shape. I then like to go round in a circle and roughly fold a little bit from the outer edge in towards the middle, until you've been round the whole circle. Then turn it over and roll the base gently so you have a tidy seam underneath and place onto the baking sheet or tray. Leave them about 2cm apart. If you like a flat teacake you can gently push down with the flat of your palm.

9. Cover the buns with a clean damp tea towel or place inside a clean proving bag, trap the air in and clip the end to keep it tight. Rest for another hour depending on the time of year and heat of your kitchen. About 15 minutes before baking, preheat the oven to 180°C fan/200°C/gas 6. When these have grown nicely to at least double you can glaze them with the beaten egg or a little sunflower oil or similar.

10. Place in the oven and bake for 15–20 minutes and turn the baking sheet or trays round halfway through for even colouring or swap the oven shelves for the 2 trays.

11. Once out of the oven, place the baking sheet or trays on cooling racks.

Enjoy cold, grilled or toasted if you dare! Maybe you have a double sided griddle and you can fill it with something to make a delicious sweet sandwich – like ice cream! Just an uninvited thought from my sweet tooth appearing here, ha ha.

Grandma's Leicester Style Fruit Bread

Intermediate

I love a fruit loaf. Slice it thick and have it heavy with butter and how
about a blob of strawberry, raspberry or apricot jam? So good! Here
I've gone to my grandmother's recipe from the 1930s for a Leicester
bread and adapted it to how I like to enjoy it. You can use plant butter,
milk and an egg substitute to make it a vegan version. Swap the dried
fruit to ones you enjoy. Or if you like the traditional lard, use it in place
of the butter. Most importantly, don't forget to set aside some time to
fully concentrate on eating your fresh slices. A cup of your favourite
tea or coffee and a book takes you to an easy, relaxing moment.

If you're looking to make this gluten free, then try a gluten free white
bread flour, using up to 50g more flour than the recipe says. And a
gluten free fast action yeast is often available where you get your
flour from. To start the recipe, soak the fruit for about 2 hours or more
before and then you'll be ready to get going. It really is worth making
it. It's always an early sell out when I take it along to markets.

This makes 2 loaves of a 1lb tin size

Ingredients

- 150g sultanas

- 75g currants

- 30g candied citrus peel

- 30g dried apricots – roughly chopped

- Water, apple juice or orange juice
  for soaking the fruit

- 450g strong white bread flour

- 6g fast action yeast

- 75g golden sugar

- ¼ tsp ground nutmeg

- 150g unsalted butter or plant butter
  (not spread) – melted, but not hot

- 130g whole milk or plant milk – at
  room temperature

- 1 large or medium egg or egg
  substitute – if you have large that's
  preferable but use what you have

- 6g salt

- Apricot jam for glazing (optional)

Extra Utensils

- Shallow bowl to soak the fruit

- Sieve

- Bowl or jug for melted butter

- Optional - Electric hand mixer or free-standing mixer with dough hook/s and large bowl

- 2 x 1lb loaf tins

- Pastry brush

Method

1. Soak the dried fruits and peel in water, apple juice or orange juice for about 2 hours. About 200g should be enough, but just enough to cover the fruit in a shallow bowl. You can do this the night before and then drain them in the morning.

2. Drain these through a sieve and leave to dry as much as possible.

3. Mix the flour, yeast, sugar and nutmeg together in a large mixing bowl or in a stand mixer bowl.

4. Prepare the wet ingredients by adding the melted butter to the milk in a measuring jug or bowl. Make sure this isn't hot, as we now add the beaten egg and we don't want the eggs to scramble. Mix briefly with a fork.

5. Pour the wet ingredients into the dry ingredients. Now add the salt and mix as you go by hand or with the dough hook of a stand mixer. Mix until smooth for about 3 minutes and then place a clean shower cap, wax wrap or cling film over the bowl. Leave the dough to sit somewhere warm for 1 hour.

6. After an hour I have to admit I didn't see as much dough growth, as in other loaf recipes, because it is an enriched dough. It makes up for it as it cooks.

Add in the drained fruit and knead it in evenly by pulling the dough up and pushing it back into itself as you go. I keep it in the bowl to do this. Some of the fruit will resist because it's an oilier mixture, but just do your best. It doesn't have to be perfect.

7. Prove the loaves in the tins. It isn't the easiest texture to shape, so I just divide it in 2 and make it into a ball by keeping as much of the top intact as possible and tucking underneath. Tuck in the loose bits and the escapee fruit that pops out. Lift it and place into the greased 1lb loaf tin and repeat for the second loaf.

8. Place a clean tea towel over the tins and put them somewhere warm to rise for roughly 45 minutes.

9. Near the end of proving time preheat the oven for at least 15 minutes to 180°C fan/200°C/gas 6.

10. Take off the tea towel and check the dough is ready. To do this, prod the dough with your finger. If the dent stays in, then prove for 10-15 minutes longer. If the dough pops straight back out, then it is ready.

11. Bake the loaves for roughly 30-45 minutes until a golden colour.

Cover loosely with greaseproof if they get too brown or turn the oven down by 20 degrees and cook for a longer time. The bottom sounds hollow when tapped if they are ready. Carefully, using oven gloves, hold the top of the loaf while you tip it upside down and hold it in the oven glove. Knock on the bottom with your knuckle and if feels hard, rather than soggy and makes a knocking noise then it's cooked. If it isn't ready, pop it back in the tin and give it an extra 5-8 minutes.

12. Put the loaves on a wire rack to cool. Take off any overly cooked dried fruit, as they can be unpleasant to eat. Glaze with just warmed apricot jam for a shiny finish, while the loaves are still warm. Enjoy your hard work, once cooled. If you've made an extra one, you may like to give this as a fresh gift to someone who needs this right now. Or you can freeze it sliced or unsliced and wrapped tightly.

It is addictive with a little butter spread over a freshly cooked slice. Wonderful! Thanks, Grandma.

Keep airtight for 3 days or it freezes well for up to a month.

Hot Cross Fruit or Choc Chip Buns

Intermediate

I have to concede that these are something I get into the swing of making over the March and April time of year and not really at any other time. It would be all or nothing and usually I made these for local produce markets. The smell would fill the kitchen, yet I would barely have any left over to share with the family. Making these for home is therefore a real treat and you get a really good result.

You can try this with gluten free bread flour and yeast. It may just need a bit of extra gluten free flour than the amount stated in the recipe. You may find that the wet ingredients affect a gluten free version, so you can be mindful of this when adding those. But give it a go. It's a lot easier than you would think and it's a real sense of achievement to bake these over Easter time. The addition of fresh apple makes a welcome change. Don't enjoy dried fruit? Make these with your preferred chocolate chips instead.

This makes 12 buns

Ingredients

- 500g strong white bread flour

- 10g fast action yeast

- 2 tsp ground cinnamon

- 70g caster sugar

- 45g unsalted butter or plant butter (not spread) – room temperature

- 100g cold tap water

- 140g whole milk or plant milk like oat or soya - gently warmed

- 2 eggs beaten or equivalent egg substitute

- 8g salt

- 120g sultanas or use 200g of your chocolate chips of choice and no fruit

- 60g citrus peel - chopped

- 1 eating apple, peeled and cut into small chunks – just before adding to the dough

Crosses Topping

- 80g plain flour

- 80g cold tap water

Glaze

- Warmed apricot conserve or marmalade without the peel

Extra Utensils

- Electric hand mixer or free-standing mixer with dough hook/s and large bowl

- Piping bag, sandwich bag or greaseproof paper made into a cone (see this recipe for details)

- Pastry brush

Method

1. Into your mixing bowl place the flour, yeast, cinnamon and sugar and mix gently until well dispersed.

2. Next add the butter, water, milk, eggs and salt and mix with a wooden spoon or on a medium speed with a dough hook for about 2 minutes. It should come together as a rough dough. I don't usually suggest adding more bread flour, but if it is very wet add a small amount like 10g-20g.

3. Again, if you've tried some other recipes in this book, you have the choice of kneading by hand or keep the dough in the electric mixer and mix on medium with the dough hook for 5 minutes. It will be wet and then get smoother. To knead by hand, add a little flour to the worktop and keep stretching and folding it for roughly 8 minutes. You can use a dough scraper or thin spatula to scrape it off the worktop and keep it coming together.

4. Time to rest the dough in a lightly oiled bowl and cover with something airtight like a clean shower cap, wax wrap or recyclable cling film. Place somewhere warm for 2 hours. Maybe less on a hot day.

5. Once about doubled in size add the sultanas, peel and apple. Knead these evenly into the dough, in the bowl. It shouldn't take very long at all.

Then place the dough in a bowl and cover with something airtight. Rest covered for another hour somewhere warm.

6. Next get your baking sheet or trays that are greased and lined. If you want identically sized buns, you can weigh the dough and divide by 12 or you can divide by eye instead.

7. Like my other recipes, I like to shape each bun by pulling the dough outwards into a flattish circle shape. I then go clockwise, folding the outer edge, bit by bit into the centre of the circle. Then turn it over and roll the base gently so you have a tidy seam underneath and place onto the baking sheet or tray.

8. These can be put on the tray about 0.5cm apart as they don't need a big gap in between.

9. Cover the buns with a clean damp tea towel or place inside a clean proving bag, trap the air in and clip the end to keep it tight. Rest for another hour depending on the time of year and heat of your kitchen. About 15 minutes before baking, preheat the oven to 180°C fan/200°C/gas 6.

10. When these have grown to about double in size you can make the crosses topping by mixing together the plain flour with the water until there are no lumps. If you don't have a piping bag

you can use a clean sandwich bag, then cut a small corner off with scissors, just before you want to pipe. Turn the nozzle upwards when you don't want the paste to seep out.

11. You can pipe the crosses as you choose. I like to go all the way across the buns, in one direction, with a little pause in between each bun. Then repeat in the other direction across each row of buns. If you want to make up your own pattern then do that. Get creative.

12. Place in the oven and bake for 15–20 minutes and turn the baking sheet or trays round halfway through for even colouring or swap the oven shelves for the 2 trays.

13. Once out of the oven, place the baking sheet or trays on cooling racks and get the glaze ready.

14. Gently warm the apricot conserve or marmalade in a small pan on the hob or in the microwave for 10 seconds in a microwavable bowl. Brush over the buns liberally and leave to fully cool down.

You can serve these up morning, teatime or supper time and you will want to dive in. I love them grilled with butter and jam for an extra treat.

Gluten Free

Gluten Free Fluffy Focaccia

Beginner

This recipe is so lovely. It's a sensation above general gluten free tin loaves. Full of Mediterranean types of flavours, with the olive oil travelling along the grooves of a puffy texture. It's perfect with heavily scented fresh herbs and flaked sea salt. Or add olives and garlic for even more flavour combinations. I do reluctantly use a teaspoon of baking powder in this and it brings such a great focaccia consistency, along with the gluten free yeast. I think you will be pleased with the result you get from this. Many who eat it will not guess that it's actually gluten free. This is best enjoyed on the day. Keep it in an airtight tin for the next day or two and gently rewarm it to soften it up.

This makes 1 focaccia

Ingredients

- 330g all-purpose gluten free flour

- 6g caster sugar

- 1 tsp baking powder

- 6g gluten free fast action yeast

- 260g tepid water – 80g just boiled water added to 180g cold tap water

- 40g olive oil

- 10g cider vinegar

- ½ tsp ground table salt

Extra Utensils

- Optional - Electric hand mixer or free-standing mixer with balloon whisk and large bowl

- 1-litre or bigger jug

- Spatula

- Baking tin – 23cm wide. Round or square

Topping

- 2 tbsp olive oil

- 4 fresh rosemary sprigs – central stick removed

- Flaked sea salt

Method

1. Prepare your round or square tin by greasing it lightly and then adding greaseproof paper to line it. It can be lined quickly by tearing off a big enough piece to fill the inside. Scrunch it up into a ball in your hand and then push it into the tin so it covers the base and comes up the sides at least 1cm. Add a small drizzle of olive oil and rub it on the paper with your hands.

2. To make the mixture, it is very quick. Start by adding all the dry ingredients, except the salt, to the large mixing bowl or electric mixer bowl. So that's the flour, sugar, baking powder and yeast. Mix together until combined.

3. Then, in another bowl or jug, put the wet ingredients of the tepid water, oil and cider vinegar together.

4. Next add the wet ingredients to the dry and as you start to mix, add the salt. Mix with a wooden spoon or the electric mixer and a balloon whisk. This will come together as a very wet mixture, almost the consistency of double cream. So, you only need to mix for a minute or two.

5. Now transfer the dough to the lined tin, using a bendy spatula to push out all of the mixture.

6. Cover the tin with a tea towel and place somewhere warm for an hour. I did this in the oven with only the oven light on and the door shut. You can place it in a warm airing cupboard or anywhere warm and out of direct heat.

7. After an hour, this very runny dough will have risen. It is quite delicate. Preheat your oven to 180°C fan/200°C/gas 6. Drizzle your olive oil over the top and put the rosemary evenly over the top too. Finish with a sprinkle of flaked salt evenly.

8. At this point I use wet hands and push my fingers in to make little dimples. It won't react like glutenous dough, so this helps to push the rosemary, oil and salt down. It will add a nice bit of texture to the surface too.

9. Place the tin into the oven and bake for 30 minutes. It should be a rich golden colour on top and baked through to the base.

When it is baked, place on a wire rack in its tin and leave to cool slightly. It can be eaten while still warm or once it's cooled. It's hard to hold back from diving into it straight away!

Gluten Free Fluffy Loaf

Beginner to Intermediate

It's a necessity for many people to have gluten free for dietary needs. So, to have a really good gluten free bread recipe in the toolbox makes life so much easier and safer. This is what I'd call a daintier loaf. For a more substantial loaf visit the buckwheat loaf recipe on page 125, which is also gluten free. What I enjoy about making this loaf is it's very easy to mix and there's no kneading required. The eating part is just as enjoyable because it has a fluffy open texture and a less grainy feel. If this is a loaf you are likely to bake frequently, you can mix the different flours and husk together as a double or triple amount. Then weigh out 400g of the mixed flours with husk each time you make this recipe for a single 2lb loaf or two 1lb ones. The bread is lovely with a thick layer of the butter of your choice and a vegetable soup. Specialist flours and husk can be bought from local millers and health food shops and some supermarkets.

This makes 2 loaves of 1lb tin size or 1 loaf of 2lb tin size

Ingredients

- 120g oat flour – you can grind oats yourself in a food processor with the chop blade

- 100g sorghum flour – this is a type of cereal grain

- 80g tapioca starch flour

- 40g potato starch flour

- 60g ground psyllium husk – not the powder

- 7g gluten free fast action yeast

- 1 tsp baking powder

- 220g of just boiled water

- 305g plant milk – coconut, oat or soya work well

- 1 tsp cider vinegar

- 1 tbsp honey or maple syrup or agave syrup

- 16g olive oil or sunflower oil

- 1 tsp ground table salt

- Sunflower or other vegetable oil of your choice to grease the tins

Extra Utensils

- Optional - Electric hand mixer or free-standing mixer with dough hook/s and large bowl

- 1-litre or bigger jug

- 2 x 1lb loaf tins or 1 x 2lb loaf tin

- Pastry brush

Method

1. Grease your chosen loaf tins, either 2 x 1lb ones or 1 x 2lb and line with a strip of greaseproof paper along the base and up 2 sides. This helps with lifting the loaf out after baking.

2. Weigh the different flours and husk into a large bowl or bowl of your electric mixer – oat, sorghum, tapioca, potato, psyllium. You should have 400g total. Add the yeast and baking powder to the flours and mix to combine evenly.

3. Next weigh all the wet ingredients into a jug. You should have the water, milk, cider vinegar, honey or syrup and olive oil or oil of your choice.

4. Add the wet ingredients to the dry mixture and as you do so, add the salt.

5. Mix with a wooden utensil or an electric mixer with paddle or balloon type whisk until it comes together. This happens quite quickly, so usually up to a minute is fine for this part.

6. Once mixed, place half of the mixture in each of the 2 tins or all of it into the 2lb loaf tin.

7. Place a clean tea towel over both tins and allow to rise somewhere warm for an hour. By this time the top will have risen slightly.

8. About 15 minutes before the end of this prove, preheat your oven to 180°C fan/200°C/gas 6. Then just before placing in the oven, brush the top of the loaf with a small amount of olive / sunflower oil.

9. To bake, put a small ovenproof dish or high-sided tin on the bottom oven shelf. Then place the bread in its tin(s) on the middle oven shelf with a gap in between them if baking 2 loaves. Carefully pour just boiled kettle water into the empty tin on the bottom shelf, between a third or halfway up. Shut the oven door and bake for about 35-40 minutes. This may be 5-10 minutes longer when baking the single larger loaf. I treated this like a cake, as I found if I opened the oven too early the top can sink down after baking. So, try not to open it before 30 minutes of baking.

10. When baked the loaf or loaves should be cooked through to the base.

11. Once baked put the loaves on a cooling rack out of their tins and allow to cool fully. Use a small metal palette knife to ease any sides that may have stuck.

12. This kept really well in an airtight container or wrapped tightly for up to 5 days. It can also be wrapped and frozen for up to a month. Perfect for stockpiling for you or for when your gluten free family or friends turn up for dinner.

Tip: you can replace 20g of the psyllium husk with flaxseed that's been milled – some people can be allergic to flaxseed, so I have not included it in the above recipe. Both of these ingredients are a binding agent and so if you enjoy flaxseed and know you are not allergic, or the person you're baking for, then give it a try.

Gluten Free Buckwheat Loaf

Beginner to Intermediate

You may be familiar with buckwheat as an ingredient in pancakes and cakes. This loaf makes a really substantial offering and the taste and texture are so welcoming to a gluten free loaf. It's really simple to make and I hope it will be a useful option to people who are gluten free and to those who aren't. It's the perfect size and softness for sandwiches.

This makes 2 loaves of 1lb tin size or 1 loaf of a 2lb tin size

Ingredients

- 450g buckwheat flour

- 60g tapioca flour

- 2 tsp gluten free baking powder

- 7g gluten free fast action yeast

- 25g ground psyllium husk

- 750g tepid water

- 20g vegetable or olive oil

- 20g maple syrup, runny honey or agave syrup

- 10g salt

Extra Utensils

- Optional - Electric hand mixer or free-standing mixer with dough hook/s and large bowl

- 1-litre or bigger jug

- 2 x 1lb loaf tins or 1 x 2lb loaf tin

Method

1. Grease your chosen loaf tins, either 2 x 1lb ones or 1 x 2lb and line with a strip of greaseproof paper along the base and up 2 sides. This helps with lifting the loaf out after baking.

2. Weigh the different flours into a large bowl or bowl of your electric mixer. Add the baking powder and yeast to the flours and stir to combine well.

3. Add the ground psyllium husk to the water. Mix well with a fork until smooth. Allow to stand for 5 minutes. In this time it will thicken.

4. Pour the wet mixture into the flours. Add the oil, your sweet syrup or honey option and salt. Then mix well, until all dry and wet ingredients are thoroughly combined. You can do this with a wooden spoon or your electric mixer.

5. Leave the mixture in the bowl, cover with a clean tea towel and let it stand for 1 hour in a warm place.

6. After this time place half of the mixture in each of the 2 tins or all of it into the 2lb loaf tin.

7. Place a clean tea towel over both tins and allow to rise somewhere warm for half an hour. By this time the top will have risen slightly.

8. About 15 minutes before the end of this prove, preheat your oven to 180°C fan/200°C/gas 6.

9. To bake, put a small ovenproof dish or high-sided tin on the bottom oven shelf. Then place the bread in its tin(s) on the middle oven shelf with a gap between them if baking 2 loaves. Carefully pour just boiled kettle water into the empty tin on the bottom shelf, between a third or halfway up. Shut the oven door and bake for 30 minutes.

10. After this time turn the oven down to 160°C fan/180°C/gas 4. And bake for 5 more minutes (smaller loaf) or 10 minutes (large loaf). The loaf will have a lovely deep golden brown colour.

11. Once baked put the loaves on a cooling rack and leave to sit there for 10 minutes before turning out of their tins or tin. Use a small metal palette knife to ease any sides that may have stuck. Let it cool fully before slicing, if you an wait that long!

This keeps really well in an airtight container or wrapped tightly for up to 5 days. It can also be wrapped and frozen for up to a month.

Index

70 / 30 wholemeal and white sourdough   29-30
Acknowledgements   130
Agave   37, 81, 122, 125
Apple   11, 108, 109, 111, 113
Apricot   37, 108, 110, 111, 114
Baking motivation   15
Brioche   65
Brioche burger buns   65-66
Buckwheat   125
Cheddar   37, 38, 48, 87
Cheese   37, 38, 41, 48, 50, 58, 59, 66, 77, 87, 89
Chef's rye blend sourdough   33-34
Chocolate   111
Ciabatta sticks or rolls   95-98
Cider vinegar   117, 119, 122, 124
Cinnamon   37, 92, 99, 101, 111, 113
Citrus peel   108, 111
Classic white sourdough   23-28
Croutons   52
Currants   108
Deep malthouse sourdough   31-32
Feta   87, 92
First-time focaccia   55-58
Flatbread   59-62, 91-94
Flavoured sourdough   35-38
Focaccia   19, 49-51, 55-58, 117-120
Food allergies   5, 23, 38, 124
Fruit   108, 111
Garlic   45, 47, 83, 86, 117
Garlic and herb milk bread twists   83-86
Gluten free   5, 9, 59, 81, 108, 111, 116-128
Gluten free   125-128
Gluten free   117-120
Gluten free fluffy loaf   121-124
Grandma's Leicester style fruit bread   107-110
Halloumi   87
Herbs   48, 52, 83, 86, 87, 94, 117
Herby sourdough croutons   52
Honey   37, 81, 82, 122, 124, 125
Hot cross fruit or choc chip buns   111-114
Inspired flatbreads   59-62
Jalapeño   35-37
Loaf of deep rye   75-78
Malt   32
Maneesh style flatbreads   91-94
Maple   122, 125, 127

Marmite   38
Mixed spice   103
My baking tips   9-12
Nutmeg   92, 108, 109
Oat   37, 59, 81, 82, 83, 90, 99, 111, 122, 124
Olive oil   45, 47, 48, 50, 51, 55, 57, 81, 82, 92, 94, 95, 97, 117, 119, 122, 124, 125
Olives   58, 87, 117
One hundred per cent wholemeal   67-70
Pizza   8, 19, 45-48, 50, 51
Pizza sauce   45, 47, 83
Plant butter   11, 59, 65, 83, 87, 99, 103, 108, 111
Potato starch   122, 124
Psyllium husk   122, 124, 125, 127
Roasted peppers   50, 87
Rolls (cobs)   41-42, 65, 81-82, 95-98
Rosemary   50, 51, 52, 55, 57, 117, 119
Rye   7, 19, 22, 23, 29, 32, 33, 35, 38, 75-78
See you later sourdough   39-40
Sorghum flour   122, 124
Sourdough cobs   41-42
Sourdough focaccia   49-51
Sourdough pizza and pizza sauce   45-48
Sourdough starter   19-22
Spelt   81, 82
Spelt flour rolls   81-82
Starter for sourdough   19-22
Sticky cinnamon buns   99-102
Stuffed loaf   87-90
Sultanas   99, 101, 102, 103, 105, 108, 111, 113
Sundried tomatoes   87
Tapioca   122, 124, 125
Teacakes for toasting   103-106
The buttie satisfier – white tin loaf   71-74
The sourdough clean-up   7-8
Tin loaf   67-69, 71-74, 75-78, 121-124, 125-128
Tips   7-8, 9-12
Utensils   7, 8, 14
Vegan   5, 11, 37, 38, 42, 48, 50, 59, 65, 75, 81, 83, 87, 99, 103, 108, 111, 122,
Wholemeal   19, 22, 23, 29, 33, 35, 37, 38, 67-69
Yeast   9, 19, 21, 22, 38, 51, 55, 57, 65, 66, 67, 69, 72, 73, 75, 77, 81, 83, 85, 87, 89, 92, 94, 95, 97, 99, 101, 103, 105, 108, 109, 111, 113, 117, 119, 122, 124, 125, 127
Za'atar   92, 94

Acknowledgements

Those people who have helped me to get this book to fruition.

Mum, those hours of standing next to you on the wobbly stool as a child. And for assisting me with the book title.

Grandmother Josephine, for documenting the history of your cooking journey.

My partner, Giles, when you think it can't be done, that always motivates me. And thanks for eating literally a ton of sourdough loaves.

My sons, for always enjoying trying anything I make and encouraging me with your ratings out of ten.

My sisters for supporting my micro bakery and all of its experimental bakes.

My friends and family and those who happily welcomed being 'beta readers' for this book.

The Free From Food Awards, for placing such an amazing award in my grasp.

The Real Bread Campaign for educating me by saying what shouldn't be in real bread, I've discovered the delights of what can be.

Customers and other businesses, who have given me well-honed feedback of what they enjoy about my bakes and the services I've provided

Sue Marriott, my mentor who showed me how to structure my work / life balance and how to make a dream goal a reality.

The Women Who, Worcestershire members and organisers who give advice and support freely.

My friends, all of whom have raised me up and believed in my abilities, at times where I didn't believe in myself.

Author

Cath Lloyd-Williams was born in 1977 in Somerset. She earned a BSc Hons in social sciences with the Open University, before becoming a family support practitioner. Cath has spent most of her life enjoying cooking and baking whilst raising two sons. In 2011, one of Cath's sons was diagnosed with a life-threatening allergy to peanuts and tree nuts, and diagnosed with asthma. Cath then changed her career to cooking and baking in local café's, gaining experience and insight into producing food for all kinds of dietary requirements. In 2019, Cath launched her own homemade food delivery business, The Doorstep Baker. She taught herself bread and sourdough baking and made every item without peanuts or tree nuts. In 2023, Cath won a Gold award at the Free From Food Awards for her classic sourdough loaf in the nut and peanut free category. She now spends her time offering baking workshops, writing recipes and selling her bakes at local farmers markets in Worcestershire, where she lives. Her debut recipe book 'The Doorstep Baker: You can make all sorts of bread' has been published independently by Cath, using recipes from her baking workshops.

Printed in Great Britain
by Amazon

3e5e31f6-a953-43a7-a785-8bfa955eba84R01